Stan Delaplane's

MEXICO

Stan Delaplane's

MEXICO

by Stan Delaplane

with Stuart Nixon

Illustrations by Antonio Sotomayor

CHRONICLE BOOKS

Printed in the United States of America

Library of Congress Cataloging in Publication Data

Delaplane, Stanton.
  Stan Delaplane's Mexico.

  1. Mexico—Description and travel—1951-
2. Delaplane, Stanton. I. Title. II. Title: Mexico.
F1216.D44   917.2'04'820924   76-14399
ISBN 0-87701-084-6

Chronicle Books
870 Market Street
San Francisco, California 94102

Contents

On Mañana Time

M E X I C O

Gulf of Mexico

Pacific Ocean

This MEXICO will read best if you take it on Mexican time. The way it was written. In small bites of six hundred words or so.

It is no brisk guide to Mexico. A little information may have slipped in by accident—the best spicy ceviche in the Republic. But it was the Indian woman cook I was writing about.

I wrote on a rocking fishing boat where Baja California ends, and there's nothing but three thousand miles of blue water until you reach The-Islands-Under-The-Wind.

In a sunny courtyard in Mexico City, beside the street where Cortez retreated on the Sad Night, I listened to the bells in the churches he built ring for the Spanish soldiers who died there. For their companions who won the final victory on this same road.

Some were written on tropical beaches of Guerrero—one in the freezing highlands of Michoacan.

With advice from house maids—"for a cold, Señor, bind slices of onion to the soles of your feet."

With misinformation that sent me on useless errands on terrible roads: "Certainly, Señor, the road is completely paved and takes you directly to Mitla." (The road was so bad that the car fell apart. I had it towed to town—which was nowhere near Mitla either.)

There are no costs. They would only be confusing. A friend in San Francisco asked me to send him seventy-five Mexican straw sombreros. I found a man who made hats. "Twenty pesos, Señor."

When I said I wanted seventy-five, he answered: "In that case, they will be forty pesos, Señor." Why? "Because it is so much more work."

In this wonderful country, time doesn't run by electronic watch. Money has values that don't relate to our flickering pocket calculators.

In Mexico I never had anything stolen. I was never cheated. I bargain. It's part of the game. But I never felt later that I paid more than a fair price.

We lived—with two small children—in houses and hotels and roadside motels. We all stayed healthy.

Maids brought us bags of delicious Mexican lemons. "It would be sinful to buy them in the market, Señora. There are so many where I live."

Waiters offered advice and sympathy on hangovers.

A truck driver stopped where I'd run out of gas. Drained some for me from his own tank.

I even made money on the Tooth Fairy. I'd stopped off inflation at ten cents at home. One tooth, one dime. In Mexico, I rewarded each lost tooth with a silver peso the size of our half dollar.

The peso is eight cents U.S. I saved two pennies and was known throughout our Mexican household as The Last of the Big-Time Spenders.

Central Mexico

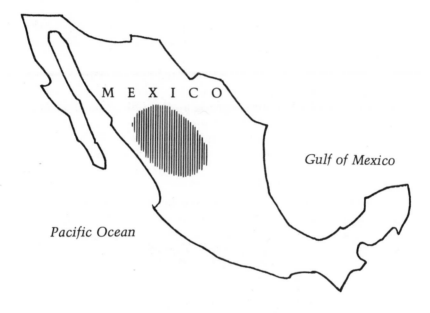

M E X I C O

Gulf of Mexico

Pacific Ocean

The French doors are open on the sunny plaza in Morelia and the maid bustles around flinging fresh sheets on the bed. No doubt Spanish Viceroys slept in this room. The Hotel Virrey de Mendoza was their summer palace.

The maid is full of information: "If you suspect someone of being a witch, watch for a light in the sky at night. Recite the 'Magnificat.' Then they must descend to earth and reveal themselves in their true human form."

She said: "If someone makes bad talk about you, get a toad. Sew its mouth up with green thread. Leave it on that person's doorstep."

Rain, Rain, Go Away!

Coatlinchán—Tlaloc was hauled away from this Aztec village to Mexico City one night. He sat here in stony silence for fourteen centuries. Then they hauled him away on a specially built truck.

As you might expect from pushing around the Rain God, it rained in Mexico City. A retaining wall went down in Tacubaya. And a Sears Roebuck building was flooded.

Don't fool around with Tlaloc unless you're carrying an umbrella!

Coatlinchán is near Texcoco. From this city on the shores of the Aztec lake, Cortez built and launched the barkentines that starved out the capital.

For some time, Mexico City has been working on moving the stone monolith that stood near Coatlinchán. No easy job. Tlaloc weighs 167 tons—probably the only thing that kept him from being destroyed by Spanish priests.

Finally they built a special road to where he stood.

They built a special trailer that cost $800,000.

They brought in enough cable to wire him down like Gulliver.

Now there was some talk that the people of Coatlinchán might not like this. You know how people are—if Washington

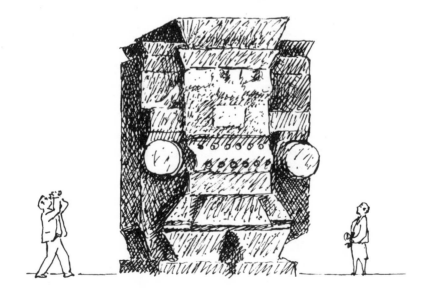

decided to move the Golden Gate Bridge and put it over the Potomac because it was kind of pretty—

So Mexico City said: "The people of Coatlinchán are very backward. They worship this idol and are superstitious. They think if we move Tlaloc the farmers won't get rain."

The people of Coatlinchán said: "That's a lie. We are very modern folks around here."

Mexico City then said: "Look, if we move Tlaloc, we'll build you a school."

The people of Coatlinchán said: "That's an awful lot of stone we are letting you have. How about throwing in a health center and a few deep wells."

"Done," said Mexico City.

Mexico City then built the road and the trailer—it carried a big advertising sign: "Goodrich tires." (I wonder who got the concession to sell space on the side of that trailer.)

They built a special steel scaffolding to get him up on the truck and out of the sand.

Apparently not everybody in Coatlinchán agreed with the deal. On one night somebody cut the scaffold cables. A box of dynamite disappeared. And there was talk of blowing up the special road.

Just to make sure, they moved Tlaloc in the dead of night.

And for further insurance, they sent an escort—1200 soldiers!

Even in the night, the word got around. And hundreds of Coatlinchán Indians lined the road to see the Rain God leave his ancient home.

There seems to be some argument about whether Tlaloc was an Aztec god. Or whether he was only for the people who carved him—the same ones who built the pyramids at Teotihuacán.

He looks a little like Richard Nixon to me. Same jaw.

There is also some question whether Tlaloc is a Rain God or a Rain Goddess. But as one Mexican scientist pointed out:

"When you are 1400 years old, what difference does it make?"

Anyway, Tlalóc was finally set up in Mexico City—but first they had to figure out how to get him off the trailer. Nobody had thought of that. They did all the engineering to get him *up* on the trailer. Then they couldn't figure how to get him down.

They finally set him up in Chapultepec Park. Where Montezuma used to walk under the ancient ahuehuete trees. And the tourists go out to see the palace where Maximilian and Carlotta lived.

It's on all the sight-seeing trips.

Wear your rubbers.

Bad Guys and Good Guys

Tres Marias—Everywhere you go in Mexico, the folk you are with will volunteer that the next village has "*mala gente*"—bad people.

So as we mounted the freeway out of Mexico City, the driver waved his hand at a collection of adobe houses and said: "*Mala gente.*"

Why are they bad? "Well, señor, when the old road ran through that village—the road that Emperor Maximilian and Carlotta rode in the royal carriage—those people made their living by robbing travelers."

Now the Mexico City-Cuernavaca doubletracked freeway goes right past the villages.

The new road was a blow to the little villages of the highlands.

If they did not live by robbing the traveler, they certainly depended on the bus stopping long enough for a quick tequila. A taco bought through the bus window.

Now cars shoot the by-pass at high speeds. Mounting the Mexican backbone for the long drop to the banana coast.

It's enough to make any people bad.

It is warm in the highlands now. The pine trees glisten in the sun, each needle a green reflecting mirror.

On the magnificent view turnouts, you can look back on the valley of Mexico. A hazy, dusty valley where the Spanish drained the great Aztec lakes.

But always above the haze, in the clear upper air, you see the snow cone of Popocatepetl.

At the top of the grade you come to the village of Tres Marias. Since the highway deserted Tres Marias, Tres Marias moved over to the highway.

There is a string of open-air, shacky little restaurants.

Oilcloth covered tables and brown Indian waitresses, all wearing the same moody look.

The old highway is only a block from the new freeway here. But most of the restaurants have moved to the new.

In 1846, that effervescent reporter Mme. Calderón de la Barca came through here and noted:

"The hills are said to be full of bandits. And the inhabitants of this village are reputed to live by all manner of robbery and thievery."

You get the idea? *Mala gente.*

From Tres Marias you can shut off the engine and let the car roll down to Acapulco, five hours away at the sunny coast.

As a matter of fact, I have ridden with drivers who did shut off the engine and coast—a process known locally as "Mexican free-wheeling."

It requires steady nerves. For both passenger and driver. For you must round some curves at high speed in order to mount short rises just beyond.

This sporting driving is usually done on the old road.

The old road has more curves than a Floradora chorus line. And it was to straighten out the way that Mexico built the new freeway.

However, the adventurous drivers prefer the curvy old road. The shut-off engine and a wild, swinging ride down the mountains.

Besides, it's free. The "freeway" costs you eight pesos.

There is wonderful back country for exploring here—with a tough, four-wheel drive car.

Get off the highways of Mexico and you are on roads built for (and used by) ox-carts. They shake a standard stock car right off the axles.

In the back country here the Indians rode with Zapata. The brass cartridges winking from full cross-bandoleers. And the tough Indian ponies going hell-for-leather through the villages. (You see a number of ruined haciendas with walls still smoke-stained from the day they were fired.)

Cortez and his conquistadors rode these highlands. Cleaning up the back country for the final assault on Mexico City in the center of the shimmering lake.

Two miles high in mountain air so thin you take it in gulps. The high country.

Barefoot Burglar

Guadalajara—A sunny morning in the Mexican highlands. While we were still having coffee, Plácido, the houseboy, came up and announced a bathroom door was locked. "From the inside, Señor."

I went down. There was a good bit of room between the door and the jamb. So I sprung it with a plastic credit card. Just like they do on TV. Plácido is mightily impressed—he thinks I'm some kind of cat burglar, I guess.

A man who sits all morning at a typewriter, staring into space, must have something going for him.

Not much crime in Mexico. The police are efficient. You are considered guilty until you can prove otherwise.

The American Consulate in Guadalajara explained this to 2000 American summer school students the other day: The life and hard times of the pothead.

Possession of marijuana gets you two to nine years.

From the time of arrest, they lock you up—no bail—while they gather evidence for sentencing. This takes six to eight months!

The Consulate gives advice. But *marijuana* is a Federal charge here—it's not like parking next to a fire plug.

The best they can do is get you a lawyer. A *marijuana-*

charge lawyer gets around $2000. There's no Escobedo ruling in Mexican courts. If you had Mary Jane in your pocket, about all your lawyer can give you is sympathy.

There's one out: If your sentence is less than five years, you can post a type of bail and head for the border. The bail fee is $400 for each year of sentence.

You still do that six to eight months waiting for sentence first.

In spite of this, they tell me there's plenty of pot drifting around. And a bearded type told me: "Man, in Acapulco I was braced by sellers four times in the first block out of the bus station."

There are thirty American men and two American women in the Guadalajara State prison as I write this. Most of them in their twenties. Most of them from California.

Mexico is much tougher than the U.S. And some Mexicans think our jail system with bail and legal loopholes is naive.

A Mexican said to me: "You catch a thief in the act. Then you let him go because the policeman didn't say the right words to him before he put on the handcuffs."

A Mexican prison is no summer cruise. But in some ways they have more regard for human feelings.

There's a restaurant service—if you have the money. The prisoner is allowed regular conjugal visits with his wife. Or

his girl friend. Or with a play-for-pay girl—if he can pay.

They feel that denying this to a prisoner would be cruel and unusual punishment.

The only trouble tourists have down here is with traffic. People drive like mad—and know their town. You sit there looking at the five-way signal. Wondering if you are going to get clobbered from the front or the rear.

Traffic police sometimes are posted on the side rather than in the center. And the other day I drove right past one. He had his hand held up—*stop*.

I put on the brakes when I saw him—on the other side of the intersection. But he only shook his head at me and waved me on.

Parking meters have come to Mexico. I don't know if they give tickets. They used to just unscrew your license plate. Take it to the police station.

You don't ignore that kind of summons.

Night Storm

San Isidro—At three in the morning I woke at a great bang of thunder. The Mexican sky was blazing with lightning. Sheets of photoflood lit the black mountains in the city.

In all the valley from Zapopán to Tláquepaque rain came hissing to the warm earth.

It was a magnificent storm: I went barefoot and opened the doors—it's warm as mother love now. The lightning leaves a memory impression. You see everything in all detail several seconds after the flash.

There was an electric feeling in the air. A sense of well being and alertness—if I had hair along the spine it would have been standing up.

Thunder filled the world. (The Aztec Gods are in the heavens again. The ships of Cortez are burning in the tropic night.)

By and by the lightning lost its power. The rain beat on steadily. I went back to bed and slept like a child.

We are in Mexico for mango time. The noblest of fruit. I make the moppets eat them hanging over the edge of the bathtub—they are that juicy.

We have a house on the hills outside Guadalajara. It's at

San Isidro Country Club, billing itself grandly as "Home of the Bing Crosby Golf World Open."

It's a new development. Crosby has a house here and, though he's not in residence, the golden name rubs 24-carat splendor on the place. San Isidro is an old, hacienda estate. The grounds are wild and wooded and tropical flowers spring up among the trees.

Jesús brings the morning mangoes. Many Mexican mothers name one boy Jesús. (I was once arrested by a cop named Jesús—[a complete mistake, mind you]—and we straightened it out over a glass of tequila.)

"Will it rain today, Jesús?"

"God knows, Señor."

That's the way our mornings begin. We have a maid who cooks a little. But Jesús only lets her do the easy things like boiling water.

Jesús is the cook and the bartender. He orders the groceries. He stocks the refrigerator. When the hot water goes off—as hot water often does in Mexico—Jesús knows where the pilot light is located out back.

I picked up the coffee pot the other morning and got an electric shock that came close to hark, the herald angels sing.

I said: "Jesús, I got a terrible shock off that coffee pot."

I thought maybe he would take it out to be fixed. But this is Mexico. He said: "Then don't touch it, Señor." Jesús knows.

On this day more than 400 years ago, Hernan Cortez fought his way into Tenochtitlán, the island kingdom on the lakes that is now Mexico City.

The Aztec king was a captive—the Spanish burned his feet to find out where the great treasure lay.

The gods were toppling down the steps of the great temple.

No wonder it stormed in the warm, garden night.

The Endless Spring

Ajijic—Two thousand Americans live on the edge of cool, gray Lake Chapala, an hour's drive from the city of Guadalajara. Summer rentals add 500 more.

Most are retired. They come here for warm climate—it's

always spring. To make the dollar stretch farther—it does even with Mexico's runaway inflation. There are two golf courses. A posh hotel—El Camino Real.

There's a lot of entertaining back and forth. Local charity drives. An American Legion post. After five years residence, you can work in Mexico. Some go into real estate or investment businesses.

You can get secure investments that pay 12 per cent. Most people here put their money into Mexico with confidence.

What's wrong with it? An American with a huge house said: "I paid $95,000 to build the house and guest house and I've had the tile up nine times to repair the plumbing.

"Finally the plumber told me: 'Don't put paper in the toilet, Señor. In Mexico we never put any paper in the toilet.' Of course that's nonsense. Friend of mine down the street built his house for $20,000 and you could flush the Encyclopaedia Britannica through his john."

An American who's been here five years said: "The first six months you get educated. When summer storms knock out the power—and that's often—the gas station can't pump gas. So you learn to fill your car every chance you get.

"Everybody can afford a maid—women love that. She

does the laundry too. Then one day she brings back everything but forgets the towels.

"You find that out just when you step out of the shower. So you dry yourself on a shirt. After that you check the laundry."

He said: "You get used to it. Just like at home I got used to looking at the morning paper to see who was on strike. Like maybe the commute bus to my office. I wouldn't change this life for anything in the world."

Life and Hard Times

Ajijic—The Hotel El Camino Real at Ajijic opened with a glorious splash. The summer Mexican rain came bucketing down. Invaded the lobby. Bar and dining room. Ruined all the new-laid rugs.

The opening of the hotel was not advertised—probably because workmen were still putting in the windows. But this is a small community—only 2000 Americans live around Lake Chapala.

On the evening of the opening, several hundred jammed into the bar. Spilled out onto the terrace. Danced to mariachi music on the postage stamp dance floor.

We came over next day for lunch. The waiter said: "I'm sorry. We are out of white fish." He said: "I'm sorry, we are out of the vol-au-vent."

He went down the menu. He ticked off the things they were out of. It was impressive. I never saw so many things that were 86ed.

The manager said: "It is difficult to open a hotel in Mexico. To get help. All our help had to be trained. All from the village of Ajijic."

He said "We trained cashiers who had never seen a cash register. We trained waiters who had never been inside a restaurant.

"While they were in training, they did well.

"When the pressure came on the other night—ah, that was something they could not bear."

He said: "*All* our cashiers quit. *All* of them." He said: "Fifty per cent of our newly-trained waiters quit. They took off their jackets. They said: 'If I had known it would be like this, I would never have started.' "

A couple of cooks quit. José Brockman, the president of Western International, said: "I have a terrible hangover. I sat up all night giving the chef brandy, persuading him not to quit."

Western International has hotels all over the world and is the biggest hotel chain in Latin America.

They are experienced. They expect disaster—and are seldom wrong. They do not lose their cool. And in a year, their hotels settle down and run splendidly.

I talked to Rudy Casparius, the senior vice president, and he said: "One thing we found in building hotels, you cannot keep an eye on your builders and, at the same time, watch the people making your furniture."

Now, while the hotel is building, Western moves the entire furniture shop—equipment, power tools, leather, lumber —inside the shell of the rising building.

Casparius said: "Then we can watch both. Before, we ran to the furniture maker's shop. To see that they were really working on our things. If we didn't, they might start on something else.

"While we were gone, the hotel workmen put the toilets in the wrong end of the building."

He said: "Now we keep an eye on both. It is the only way."

We stayed for a night. They are large, well-appointed rooms with heavy mahogany and cowhide furniture.

Everything worked. (I'd brought my Swiss Army knife with many blades, figuring I'd have to screw something back on. I have repaired toilets all over Mexico. While the house engineer stood by admiring my work.)

But everything worked. The shower head adjusted. The water was hot. The mirror did not fall off the wall.

Casparius said: "The flood and the carpets did cause us a lot of concern. But we've opened many, many hotels. And when you've done that in Mexico, you can face a firing squad and refuse the blindfold."

A Peso Here

Chapala—A sunny day on the tailored golf course beside Lake Chapala. The daily golfers are on their appointed rounds.

Thousands of Americans have packed it in as far as the

U.S. is concerned. Stacked arms. Finished with engines. They live in Mexico.

Getting used to Mexican customs is the hurdle. One of them told me: "When you get used to *mordida*—the bite from every official you do business with—you will have solved most of Mexico."

He said: "We go up to the border every six months to renew our tourist papers. We load the station wagon: Cake mix. An electric heater. Things we can't get in Mexico.

"Now you can take a day or two while they figure out what comes in free, what pays duty. Or you can give the Customs Officer $5 or so. On your way.

He said: "Forget your ideas that such things are bribes. The *mordida* is oil. Officials here are poorly paid. They are expected to make something on the side."

He said: "You could look at it this way: The Customs man is not paid enough. So he collects the duty you would have paid. Thereby bringing his salary up to normal."

There is a sharp division on the subject. Another American said: "The *mordida* system is on its way out. Don't encourage it."

Another said: "The *mordida* makes all the difference in the world. Why, at home I had to get twelve building permits for a hotel. It took me almost a month. Inspectors. Papers. Lawyers."

He said: "Here I am building a house. My lawyer says: "Well, we'd better give a thousand pesos to so-and-so. Then you get the electrical thing right away. Then there's so much for this guy.' "

He said: "I get the whole thing done. Less money. Less fuss. Everybody's happy!"

Among the wives here, the main subject is maids. An American woman said: "I couldn't afford a maid at home. Now I have two—I get a couple more when we have a party."

She said: "But there are problems you never dreamed of. If you have a young maid, she is certain to get pregnant. Then you are involved with looking after *her*. Pre-natal care. Who takes care of the baby?"

She said: "If you have older maids, there is always sickness in the family. Her father dies. Her brother breaks his leg. There's no end to it. And you take on some of the responsibility."

The Garden of Eden has its problems. Always some snake selling apples.

An American man said: "Well, I get to play golf every day. And I live far cheaper. My wife has two maids. The houseboy washes my car every day."

He said: "I own a house I bought for $20,000 in 1970. I pay $60 a year taxes on it. I don't pay *any* income tax. I think I've adjusted. Not everybody can you know."

A Mexican said: "North Americans are all full of moral rights and wrongs. They don't see what we do in Mexico is try to get along together."

He said: "Look. A motorcycle cop stopped me the other day—I was going pretty fast. I said: 'I'm sorry. My wife wants a trip to New York. I was thinking of something else. Here's thirty pesos for the fine. OK?'

"He said: 'It's a serious infraction. You went like the wind.'

"I said: 'OK. Fifty pesos.' "

The Mexican said: "The North American would want to go to court. Bother the judge. And, in the end, it would cost the taxpayers much more."

Dust on My Knuckles

Chapala—The Mexican day dies grandly in the central highlands. Rain clouds tower in the sky. The sun spouts blood and fire and Spanish gold. There's faraway thunder. Like the boom of brass cannon.

Night comes on Lake Chapala. The mountains are black cutouts against the last light from the West. Then comes the rain.

I said: "I'll get the martinis."

I got up and my trick back went—pop! I fell back in the Mexican cowhide chair.

"I've been done in by demon rum," I said. For three days I've been walking around bent over like an orangutan. They talk poetically here of Mexican "dust on your heart."

I have dust on my knuckles.

When my back goes out, we prop it up with a kind of saddle. It straightens it out and keeps it that way.

Only thing is I didn't bring the bracer. We are in the business of getting it shipped down. A most complicated affair.

A friend in nearby Guadalajara said: "The problem is that it has to clear Customs. Now if you'd brought it in, nothing to it. But when it's shipped in, they have to send notices and all kinds of things."

He said: "It might be a week or two before you get it."

Life and hard times in a Mexican scatter: A mosquito got in the other night. When my wife woke, she had a dozen bites.

They must have itched like fury. She shouted at the moppets.

I said: "Can I have more coffee?" (The maid's day off.)

She said: "Can't you get it yourself?"

I went out on all fours. I got the coffee. I came back and blew the dust off my knuckles.

She said: "We've got to do something about flies and mosquitoes."

We are in a magnificent house, overlooking the lake. It is well screened. But I cannot get a maid or houseboy to keep them closed.

I said to the houseboy: "Plácido, keep the screen doors closed." I said in English: "*Or I'll cut your throat, ear to ear.*"

Plácido said: "With all pleasure, Señor."

He went out on the patio. He left the door open. I went over on my hands and knees and closed it.

The moppets said: "Will you really cut his throat?"

I said: "If I can get unkinked enough to reach it."

We are picking up practical medicine.

A dab of ammonia takes some of the itch out of mosquito bites. (We tried to get some antihistamine lotion. I heard that was good. But I can't locate it yet.)

If your child wets the bed, there's an herb that cures it. It grows wild here.

The maid said: "You cook it in a little water. Give it to the child for nine days. After nine days, the child is cured."

Plácido's idea of mosquito control is to leave the doors open all day. Then—before he goes—he closes the doors and squirts the whole house with a pump gun filled with fly killer.

It smells awful. It makes your eyes water. It drives you out of the house. It ruins the taste of the evening martini.

We went into the big supermarket in Guadalajara. I bought some Press-the-Button bug killer. It is great. It *murders* flies. You can see them shot down—plop.

I crawled around and sprayed the whole house. Plácido was impressed. He said: "That is better than my pump gun, Señor."

He went out the back door, humming a little Mexican love song. He left it wide open.

The 'Little Now'—and Then

Jiutepec—Coffee comes *"ahorita"*—the "little now." Which means right away but doesn't necessarily work out that way.

In the sunny highland Mexico morning, *ahorita* can mean a lot of things besides right away.

"*Ahorita*. Señor. I'll bring it."

"I've waited ten minutes, Señorita. I'm quite faint."

"The cook has not arrived, Señor. When he comes . . ."

"When do you expect him, Señorita?"

"Ah, *ahorita*, Señor. God willing, he comes *ahorita*."

Trying to rush and push and change Mexico is a sure way to frustration.

Life swings along at an easy pace. Inevitably, what you want will come is the way they look at it. Or else it won't.

At my house, the hot water tank has gone cold. The housekeeper-cook nods. She expected it.

"The tank of gas is exhausted."

"Can we buy another?"

"Yes, Señor, why not? I'll telephone *ahorita*."

"When will it come?"

"Tomorrow, Señor. God willing, it comes tomorrow."

Well, I have a cunning idea. How to keep from running out of hot water.

"When you order, Señora, buy *two* tanks of gas."

"But you can only put in one, Señor."

"The other is for a reserve. When the new one is gone, we put in the reserve, see? Then we don't run out of hot water."

The housekeeper will do it. But she doesn't see it.

What she sees is a lot of fussing around.

She thinks: "How curious these gringos are!"

In Mexico City, Bill Shanahan ran the Mexico City News. In English language—though Mexican typesetters come up with some interesting mistakes.

He said the people who have the most trouble are American managers of American companies in Mexico. Explaining to the home office how things work in Mexico.

At one time, Shanahan worked for the giant, world-wide American Mine and Smelting Co. in the silver town of Taxco.

The New York office wrote in an irritated way: "Since labor is cheap in Mexico, tell us why it is that in Taxco it costs us more to drive a mine shaft than anywhere else in the world?"

Bill's boss in Taxco said to Bill: "Very well. Write them this letter:

"*Paragraph*: You want to know why it costs more to drive a shaft in Taxco than anywhere else in the world?

"*Paragraph*: In most parts of the world, people want to improve their social and economic position. Not so in Taxco.

"*Paragraph*: In Taxco, people work as a pastime between fiestas of which there are seldom fewer than two every month. When they work, they work slowly, anticipating the fiesta.

"*Paragraph*: There is also the cost of dynamite. Each village competes to have the biggest, loudest fireworks with the biggest boom. Nothing equals our dynamite for this purpose. More dynamite goes into fireworks than goes into the shaft.

"*Paragraph*: This increases costs and makes it more expensive to drill a shaft in Taxco than anywhere else in the world.

"*Paragraph*: Very Truly Yours."

Mail from Mexico goes swiftly and efficiently. But once when I was late with copy, I impressed the urgency on a small town postmaster. He thereupon held it fourteen days on suspicion.

I tried to explain this to the American editor by mail. It

sounded so nonsensical he suspected I was loaded and covering up.

Firecracker Holiday

Puebla—There are so many holiday fiestas in Mexico that local newspapers run daily and monthly lists.

There are local fiestas. National holidays. Religious fiestas. Days of pilgrimages. There also seem to be personal fiestas. The place where my shoes are being repaired was closed the other day.

"The shoemaker has gone to his town for the fiesta," said the lady next door. She has a table set up in the street and serves light lunches directly through the kitchen window. It is a cottage industry.

"When does he return, Señora?"

"Ah, who knows, Señor? Next week. Or the week after.

It is warm now in Mexico. I can go barefoot.

This is a national day of fiesta. Here in Puebla, on this day more than a hundred years ago, the Mexicans defeated the French invading army of Napoleon III. (The Foreign Legion fought in Mexico.)

The United States was engaged in the Civil War.

The French lost the battle of Puebla. But later they were able to put the Archduke Maximilian on the throne as Emperor of Mexico.

He stayed until 1867. When the French pulled out, the Mexicans shot him on the Hill of Bells on a lonely plain outside Querétaro.

He gave the firing squad some gold pieces to shoot straight.

On days of fiesta Mexico shoots fireworks. They are excellently done. Whole scenes of pageantry are wired to wooden frames—fused to go off in sequence.

The entire battle scene of Puebla flames in technicolor over the tree-shaded, great square. Turning (as the fuses reach the right powder charges) to the red-white-and-green Mexican flag with the eagle perched on the cactus.

Rockets stream fire through the hot Mexican sky. Bombs explode over the grey-stone cathedral. Firecrackers go bang! in the street.

It is very Spanish—something like you see during religious holidays in the great square at Salamanca. With more color. Like Mexican food. A little more hot sauce.

On the Cinco de Mayo, the schools, banks and offices close. And in the *pulquerias*—(where they sell the beer-strength ferment of the cactus)—the Indians get drunk as lords.

The military band plays in the wrought-ironwork stand in the center of the plaza. And the townspeople circle the walks slowly—boys in one direction, girls in the other.

As they pass, the boys make polite little comments:

"St. Peter must have lost the keys. For here is a little angel escaped from heaven."

In the cantinas, the street singers—the *mariachis*—play for tips, for the sake of music and for the fiesta. Guitar music with the swing of a country dance.

"Why dost thou abandon me, woman?
"Just because I am poor
"And have the misfortune
"To be already married."

(That *is* a problem. A couple of problems.)

"Three vices I possess,
"And I have them with all their force.
"To get drunk and to gamble.
"And the other is to fall in love."

(He's got *everything* going.)

The general who beat the French here so many years ago, was Ignacio Zarragoza.

Napoleon III turned out to be the Bad Guy. When the U.S. got through with the Civil War, they reminded him of the Monroe Doctrine. The U.S. had a big, tough veteran army with four years of war behind it.

Napoleon got the idea. The French occupation troops sailed from Vera Cruz. And the Mexicans stood Maximilian up on the Hill of Bells.

They weren't shooting firecrackers.

The Better the Cure

Oaxaca—"I came down here fifteen years ago," said the Texas banker. "Incurable ulcers is what they told me in Dallas.

"I had two operations and all the best doctors.

"I went down in the jungles, near Acapulco—I always liked hunting and you can shoot big cats and pig—for a rest.

"One of the Indians saw I was pretty sick. He stripped some bark from a tree—they sell it in all the herb markets. Made a kind of tea of it. I took it for two weeks and was completely cured. I had a checkup back home and they confirmed it."

The herb seller is a busy man in the street market. The tree barks, plants and seeds come from ancient times.

The Aztecs had great botanical gardens. And a complete guide to plant medicine was uncovered a few years ago in the Vatican library. It had been prepared by Aztec medicine men and sent home by the first priests in the New World.

Cortez was treated for a head wound by Indian doctors.

The Mexican lemon that looks like a lime is used for colds. An American who has lived here many years told me:

"If I get a cold, my Indian major domo has a lot of lemons squeezed into hot water. He has me soak my feet in it. I don't know why but it seems to work. Better than aspirin."

Mexico is a corn country as it was in the days of the Aztecs. Tortillas are standard bread of the Republic—though bakery bread (and not as good) has some status value.

The diet of corn and beans lacks some vitamins. But these are supplied by *pulque*, a milky, lightly fermented drink from the juice of the maguey. The spiky, green-blue century plant that grows in cultivated rows all over the plateau.

It is so important that the Aztecs had more than four hundred *pulque* gods. And there are specialized bars—*pulquerias*—where they sell nothing but *pulque*.

For us it has an unpleasant smell and a sour taste. But they say you can acquire a feeling for it. If you keep at it long enough.

There are herbs for headaches and herbs that stop bleeding—the accidental cut of the machete is a common wound in the country where this blade is the all-purpose tool.

There is an herb to restore lost virginity. The state of pure maidenhood is regarded as an essential of marriage.

There are herbs for insect bites. For the heart, the liver, the kidneys and probably for flat feet.

There are herbs for love. Slip a little of this in his *pulque* and he is soft as tortilla dough. Clang, clang. Wedding bells.

Mescál, made from maguey here in Oaxaca, is a cure for colds. "Drink it hot with lemons."

Mescál is a strong distilled liquor. It gives you a hangover. But it also cures the hangover. Along with the cold.

There are witches—*brujas*. And sorcerers—*hechizeros* —who can effect cures.

Prayer has cured many. The churches of Mexico are

hung with little offerings for cures. The part of the body cured is made of silver—they sell them in little shops. And they are hung in the church. Tiny hearts. Tiny legs.

There are also home-made paintings of recoveries by prayer. The cured person paints himself on the sick bed with the saint who interceded. He takes it to the church and it is hung there.

There is a cane sugar alcohol made here which cures a variety of things. It is clear as water. Rated 92 per cent pure alcohol. A number of people drink it with Coca-Cola. They say it cures *anything*.

It is powerful. Maria, who cooks my *enchiladas*, rubs it on her rheumatic knee. It makes it limber as a willow.

Old as the Hills

Oaxaca—Though every guide in Mexico has a close friend who runs a silver factory (at extraordinarily cheap prices, naturally)—nobody will take you to an antique factory. Where they make idols for the tourist trade.

The antiques are sold in the market place.

The lady sells new antiques and old antiques.

The new dolls are gray stone and freshly carved. The old antiques have been weathered and the noses chipped off.

The lady makes no difference in the sales pitch.

"This ancient one, Señora? With the chipped nose and the hand broken?"

"Antique, Señor. Dug up in the hills by the Indios."

"And this one, all nice and shiny, Señora?"

"The same, Señor. All pure antiques."

There is a lot of real pre-Columbian art around Mexico. And a thriving black market in it—Mexico has stiff laws about exporting such things.

A great scandal came up a few years ago. It was discovered that a New England museum held a quantity of stuff pulled out of the sacred wells in the Maya country.

A good deal of the real thing, they say, is being dug out of mounds now in the wild country back of Acapulco.

Then there is the manufactured stuff in the market.

The art of antique manufacture goes back a long, long way. An expert on such things told me:

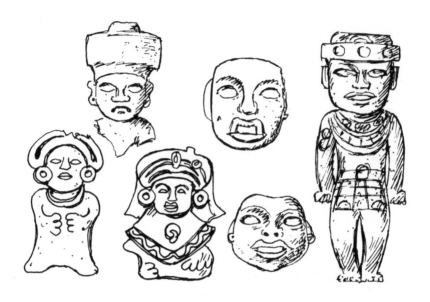

"When Scott was in Mexico City—during the Mexican-American war of 1847—one of his generals took a weekend down in Oaxaca. That was long before they discovered the famous tombs and articles of Monte Albán.

"Anyway, this general was an amateur archaeologist. He bought up several barrels of figures and broken plates and idols. He shipped them back to Washington.

"They lay around the Smithsonian Institution for years.

"About 10 years ago, somebody got them out and started to classify them. About three-fourths of them were fakes.

"When you think there were no tourists then—there weren't even roads—you wonder who they sold them to."

The expert said the curious thing was that you could buy the real thing for the same price as the fakes.

"And you can hardly tell the difference. They are made in the same way by the same kind of people.

"The Indians are always plowing up some real, ancient figure. They sell it in the market. And the market dealer probably gets it for less than he has to pay for a manufactured antique. After all, with the real thing there's no labor cost involved.

"So when you go to the market, maybe you're looking at two or three out of ten or fifteen that are genuine. But how do you know?"

In our patio we have a number of antiques. They are on brick ledges. Fearsome gods looking down on the morning chocolate. (Did they look down on other chocolate breakfasts? Or were they soaked in chocolate and then buried to give that antique, brown color?)

They have stiff headdresses and look like the figures in the rare Aztec codices. They are pitted and pocked and broken artistically.

Then there is another fellow. He is holding a pot like a bartender shaking up a shaker of martinis.

His nose is artistically snapped off.

But they forgot to age him. He looks brand new.

For the new ones in the market, the lady asks the same as for the old ones.

However, when she discovered I preferred the old ones, the price went up:

"Because they are pure antiques, Señor."

"But so are the nice new ones—antiques too, you said."

"Ah, Señor, but the others are purer. *All* pure antiques but some are purer than others."

A Chair in the Sun

Cuernavaca—The Mexico City papers arrive at a fashionable 9:30 in the morning—more or less. The boy sails them over the brick wall. The pages fly all over the yard. And I imagine gathering them up is excellent for the waistline.

The mail also comes over the wall—the postman toots a little whistle to let you know. You then go out and look in the garden. Something like an Easter egg hunt.

Sometimes you find a letter several weeks old. You learn all sorts of interesting things. That it's too late to do anything about it anyway.

In the town of Cuernavaca, in the great shady plaza and in the bustling street market, life is lively.

We sit at the tables, under the awnings at Casa Cárdenas. It is a delicatessen and luncheon place. It looks on the sunset pink stone palace built by Cortez.

In the center of the plaza there is a brown stone statue of a general who fought for Zapata.

The beer comes in ice-cold glasses.

An ancient Indian lady is selling shawl *rebozos* in a rainbow of colors. She lays them out one by one. She pays no attention to—"But I don't want a *rebozo*, Señora."

"Pure wool, Señor. Very handsome."

A small boy selling Chiclets joins the party around the table. (*All* small boys in Mexico sell Chiclets and I wonder who they sell them to.)

"No, *muchacho*. No Chiclets."

That is all right with the boy. He just likes to stand there and watch me drink beer. He stares at me. Eyeball to eyeball for the next half hour.

The old lady pulls out another *rebozo*.

"This one in red. Made by hand." (Not true. They are run up by machine. The Indian lady is selling on commission—plus what she can add to the price.)

The Indian lady pulls out another. "This one in blue, Señor. I am only making a living. What are a few little *pesitos* to you."

On the edge of the sidewalk, three mixed dogs have sat down and are giving me a friendly grin. Tourists often toss them leftovers. And they have Casa Cárdenas on their beat.

An antique begger shuffles up mumbling a pious, "For God's sake—"

In the plaza, the instant photographer sets up a fullsize,

realistic horse. Saddle, rifle and enormous *sombrero*. You mount the horse. Put on the *sombrero*. Wave the rifle.

The picture is done in five minutes. There you are, riding with Zapata in the Revolution.

The morning tourists are arriving from Mexico City to see the Cortez palace. Armed with guide books and cameras. (One of them took *my* picture with the old Indian woman. I would like to hear what he says back home when he shows the slides.)

The Chiclet boy is still staring at me. Two feet away. Eyeball to eyeball.

The man with the lottery tickets comes by. We buy a piece on the half million peso drawing. A lunge at unbelievable luck and prosperity. All for a few pesos in a day in the sun.

Assistant to the President

Cuernavaca—"One of the problems of business in Mexico," said the American resident, "is the assistant system.

"You open a hotel and hire a manager. Immediately he hires an assistant manager. That is usual in all hotels. But in the hotel here, the manager turns over all his work to the assistant —proving he is too important to see if the maids are working and the plumbing is maintained.

"If the assistant job is big enough, the assistant hires an assistant. Proving that *he* is too important to look at the plumbing.

"So eventually, the management job gets down to somebody who is not important enough to hire an assistant. And when you get down that far, the person is not top caliber. Or is paid so little, he doesn't care."

My household is full of assistants. My household is run by Manuel. He is the major domo and gardener. Administrator, shopper and husband of Maria who cooks.

Immediately after we moved in, Manuel hired a boy to assist him in the garden.

"The pool needs attention," he said.

Pool work is interesting. He has an oversized net on a long pole. With this he fishes minor floating debris from the surface. Once in a while he goes down and gives the assistant some instructions.

Maria hired herself an assistant. She is a spindly young girl, armed with a mop. She mops down the entire house which is red-tiled.

The mop is not too clean. I have been unable to saw off the idea that soap and a change of water in the bucket would improve things.

She mops steadily. The idea seems to be to cover the acreage. You can walk on the floors barefoot immediately and your soles are the color of soot.

I would show these to Maria. But I am sure she would suggest I wear shoes. "Because floors are dirty, Señor. Ah, yes, that is why they make shoes."

I have no assistant. So must have lost a lot of status in the scatter.

I rate with the lady who comes once a week to assist with the laundry. She has no assistant. She rubs the laundry on rocks. The seams of one shirt and one pair of pants have come out.

"They were badly sewn," said Maria critically.

She will fix them. "Don't occupy your mind with it, Señor."

I have an idea she will get an assistant for the sewing.

In the shady plazas downtown there are uniformed men to watch your parked car—sort of assistant traffic police. They wear polished badges and natty uniforms.

Most of them have boy assistants. The uniformed man sits under the shade trees while the boy directs you into a parking place. Two bangs with the fist on the back fender—keep backing. One bang—stop.

When you get ready to go, the uniformed man comes out briskly.

He whistles. Holds up a hand to traffic. Waves you on. Accepts and pockets the tip.

"Gracias, Señor."

The assistant gets a little. Plus experience. I suppose all the assistants get the same advice I used to get as an assistant.

"Look at the job opportunities! The experience! What do you mean you want a raise!"

The man who delivers the butane gas tanks has an assistant. The boy assistant struggles through the yard with the heavy tank. The chief collects the money and gives him the receipt.

I am the only person in the household without an

assistant. Maria passes by—to look in on *her* assistant.

"How does it go?"

"*Mucho trabajo, poco dinero*—much work, little money, Maria."

"Poor thing," said Maria. I think she means it.

Dow Jones Average

Cuernavaca—Market report from Cuernavaca, Mexico: Chickens, up 2 pesos; tomatoes, up 1 peso; trading brisk with futures uncertain.

The family shopping is done by Manuel. Gardener and administrator. Philosopher and husband of Maria, the cook.

Life in Cuernavaca is a mystery. And Manuel is not doing anything to clear it up.

"Don't occupy your mind with it," he said. In other words—leave it to Manuel.

Manuel has a lot of plates in the air. We tried shopping the colorful street market the first few days.

Manuel looked over the purchases with a kind of pity. He asked the prices and shook his head sadly.

"Naturally, the tourist pays more," he said.

He struck a pose that I find is a part of the stage

directions: He steps one step backward. Spreads his hands dramatically and hunches up his shoulders. His face shows resignation—with a "what-can-you-do-about-it?" look.

A culinary priest hearing your pitiful confession.

Next day, we sent Manuel shopping. His face beamed with satisfaction.

He came home with the groceries. The tomatoes had gone up a peso. The 10-peso chicken up five.

I mentioned this diffidently.

"These are better," said Manuel firmly. "Prices have gone up."

He took the quick step backward. Spread his hands and got that "what-can-you-do?" look.

A little later I heard him humming in the garden.

A few days later it was reported to me that Manuel was not bringing home any change.

"Ask him for an accounting," I said. "Tell him I need it for taxes."

That evening Manuel spoke to me privately. He seemed sad.

"The Señora does not trust me," he said.

"Not so, Manuel," I said. "It's just that women want to know what it costs to run a house."

Well, said Manuel, if the Señora gave him 20 pesos yesterday, that was what he spent.

"But she gave you 50 pesos the day before."

"Ah, that was the cost. Prices are high," he said.

He took a quick step backward. Spread his hands and slipped on the mask of resigned sadness.

Next day—under some prodding—he disgorged two pesos in change. From a 30-peso budget.

Under further questioning, he had a list. He added and subtracted. And when the pork chops didn't add up, he tacked the missing pesos onto the price.

I thought: "How I wish I had this man to do my expense accounts!"

The day after, we did our own shopping. The tomatoes, chicken and pork chops returned to their original prices.

Both Maria and Manuel looked over the fodder. They pronounced the tomatoes over-ripe. The chicken! Manuel took a quick step backward. Spread his hands and assumed the usual expression.

The pork chops—Maria took them and put them in the garbage can. She would not let me poison myself, she said. She cooked some delicious *enchiladas verdes*.

In the morning, I gave Manuel a handful of pesos and the shopping list. I could hear him singing in the garden. It's a happy household.

Sunday's Child

Cuernavaca—The Mariachis' Mass begins at 11 o'clock in the ancient Cathedral that Cortez built on the hill above his palace at Cuernavaca after the conquest. *Mariachis* are the street musicians of Mexico. Traditionally there must be guitars, violins, and a brassy trumpet. Other combinations of instruments are not *mariachis*.

Some years ago, Bishop Sergio Mendez Arceo decided that the church music should be played by musicians of the people. He began the Mariachis' Mass and people come from all over Mexico to hear it.

Cuernavaca is a flowery town at 5000 feet. It's always spring. The sun bounces off broadleaf mirrors of banana plants. Jacaranda trees are a shower of lilac. Flamboyant trees become parasols of Chinese red flowers.

There are Indian laurels. Great *ahuehuete* trees. Cortez sat under such a tree and wept on "The Sad Night" as he retreated from the Aztec capital.

There's a great shady flagstone courtyard outside the Cathedral and it is filled with merchants.

Boys sell armloads of necklaces made of red seed beads and carved wood. A woman with a hot kettle fries *churros*, a type of long doughnut.

A seller of cotton candies displays bright pink puffs on a 15-foot pole stuck in the air.

The girl moppet has $9 U.S. that is burning a hole in her pocket. She says: "I can get those beads for 5 pesos. Will you change my dollars?"

I answer: "Change your money here? Don't you remember how Jesus ran the money changers out of the temple? I'll give you 12.35 pesos to the dollar."

She says: "Dad! The banks give you 12.49."

I say: "This is Sunday, Señorita. The banks aren't open. I have to make a living."

I say: "Look, Señorita, the hotels only give 12.40 but for you I am going to make it 12.42."

It is a good day to go to church.

The Mass begins with the *mariachis* playing *Sanctun*. The Bishop in a green surplice takes the procession to the altar flanked by three in white and gold, led by altar boys carrying lighted candles.

There are six *mariachis*—white shirts and black trousers trimmed in silver. Three guitars. Two violins. One trumpet. The trumpet player doubles on a kind of bongo drum three feet high.

There's a lead singer on a podium. And under his direction, everybody joins in. The acoustics are excellent under a high vaulted ceiling. The doors are open. And sunlight filters through the great windows and brown-and-beige squares of Mexican glass.

The Bishop spoke in Spanish. I couldn't get it all but at one point he offered a prayer for the poor and for foreigners, which I thought covered me.

Outside the courtyard the merchants wait for the exodus. And when we came out the boy with the seed bead necklaces has reduced his price from 10 pesos to eight.

I say: "OK." But when I hand him a 10 peso bill, he says: "I have no change. Look, Señor. Take two for 12."

I say: "OK." I give him a 10 and 5.

He says: "Señor, this is terrible. I don't have change for that either. Take three and give me 15 for the three."

I turn him over to the girl moppet. She has beaten him down to three for 10 and is still arguing when I snatch her away for lunch.

The Linguist

Cuernavaca—At dawn, a series of bombs burst over the church, the beginning of a day-long bombardment. An off-key (but enthusiastic) bugle is blowing on the hillside.

Today we honor the saint of the house-builders.

The Holy Cross will be carried to homes under construction and the project blessed.

There will be roast goat and plenty of *pulque*. In Mexico, the saints like a fiesta with plenty of boom.

We are invited to an American party. The major attraction is a world traveler and bon vivant. His credentials are stated by telephone..

"He speaks seven languages fluently."

I always wonder why they speak *seven* languages. And always "fluently." Why not eight? Or six. And maybe brokenly.

Also, why is this an attraction? I only speak English fluently. So his fluency is lost on me. After English I can limp brokenly through taxi and restaurant words.

I can say to the fluent guest in Japanese: "Left. Right. Stop here."

I can say "caviar and vodka" in Russian.

I can say in Italian: "Where is the gentlemen's lounge."

I can say, "How are you?" in Tahitian. "More Coffee" in Kitchen Mexican. "Don't hang up the telephone," in French. "More beer," in German.

This gives me seven languages. Not fluently. But a start.

I don't think *anybody* speaks seven languages fluently.

In the United States, a guest must appear at parties a half hour later than the invitation reads. "Cocktails at 6:30." Show up at 7.

In Mexico, it is customary to come anywhere from one

to three hours later. Or maybe not at all. It is very relaxed. Sometimes there is no party.

A couple of years ago I was invited to an enormous party.

"You *must* come," said the host. He mentioned the guests. Presidents of big companies. Politicians of great influence. Social leaders.

I said I was sick—I really was. I was laid out like a wet shirt.

"But you are the guest of honor!" he cried.

I got out of bed. Took an aspirin and began polishing my seven languages.

At the correct time, I tottered into the hotel. Nobody—including the manager—had heard of the great party. I ran into the host by accident. He was loading up in the bar.

"The party?" he said vaguely. "Oh, we had to call that off. Something came up—"

The bombs in honor of St. Evenzia (the cook cannot write but that is the way it sounds) are bursting in air. When they go off, all the dogs within five miles bark.

Two dogs go with this household. "To keep away thieves."

We also have two cats and five kittens. We have a rooster, bought for $1. He was a bargain and is being fattened for a finer day.

There are burros across the ravine. A burro in the morning gives out an agonizing sound. Like a pipe organ if you stepped on all the discordant keys. Is the burro in pain? Or greeting the fiesta? No one knows but the burro.

"Today everybody gets drunk," says the gardener. Some fiesta!

In the soft night, the rockets rise furiously. Trailing fire and bursting in flashes of blue light.

I have not become fluent in Spanish. I have become reckless with the verbs.

I keep trying until something happens. Odd things happen, too. I keep getting taxis I didn't ask for. I must be saying something wrong. And fluently, too. The bill for un-ordered taxis is fierce.

However, if you want to be the life of the party—

Call Operator 33

Cuernavaca—The Mexican telephone has laid more tourists low than the internal discomfort known as "Monte-zuma's Revenge."

Curiously, our calls to the United States go through like hot tortillas.

When we tinker with the teléfon inside Mexico: *"Tel-éfonista!* Señorita! Please! Please!

The señorita *teléfonista* does not care to answer. Or if she answers, she must be courted with fair words.

From Cuernavaca to Mexico City, we have direct dial-ing. Dial "925." Then dial the Mexico City number. There must be no hesitation between "925" and the Mexico City number. Else the tender line of communication is lost.

I am dialing the great Hotel Del Prado. Chrome-and-glass pleasure palace of the visiting tourist. Everybody speaks English. Except—

"*Si, Señor*. This is the Del Prado."

"Can you connect me with Señor Lopez, please."

"*No, Señor*. I am sorry I cannot do that."

"Why not, Señorita?"

"Because this is the sixth-floor maid."

"Señorita, perhaps you can get the *teléfonista*. So I can be connected with Señor Lopez.

"*No, Señor*. I cannot do that."

"Why is that, Señorita?" (Politeness is straining at the ragged seams.)

"Because the phone is discomposed, Señor. All long-distance calls are coming into the sixth floor and we cannot change them."

That *is* a problem.

For many years we telephoned the U.S. with high hopes the call might go through some time that day.

Now we dial "09" and are immediately picked up by a bilingual operator.

The call goes through in five minutes. Often less.

However, there are nostalgic hangovers of the old days.

"Call Operator 33 in San Francisco," says the message.

"Ah," says the *teléfonista* triumphantly, "there *is* no Operator 33 in San Francisco."

"But that is the message you gave me, Señorita."

"That is what the San Francisco operator said, Señor."

"Then why not try it?"

"Because no Operator 33 is listed."

The Mexican *teléfonista* takes no responsibility for what some other operator (irresponsible, naturally) says from San Francisco.

The Mexican telephone is a blend of two phone systems. At one time, Mexico had system Ericcson and system Mexicana. Completely separate.

The two were hooked together a good many years ago. But it was a rocky marriage. They never really got along. For a long time, it was better to phone only Ericcson numbers if the original phone was Ericcson. And Mexicana-to-Mexicana was more fruitful than crossing the line.

Now Teléfonos de Mexico has straightened out crossed wires.

And all that is required is to stay straight with the touchy *teléfonista*.

We throw in "*Señoritas*" with flowers in our voice. We give her a "*muy buenas dias*" and plenty of "*por favores.*"

If the number is wrong, we apologize for being clumsy.

If we are cut off in mid-*conferencia*, we imply that we jiggled the switch. Or made some other mechanical blunder. We humble ourselves and do not ask for clearer lines. Even though there is a background of five other conversations.

By phoning collect, we discovered there *is* an Operator 33 in San Francisco. But the Mexican *teléfonista* was pretty sharp with me about it.

She implied I had personally left it off the list.

Time on My Hands

Cuernavaca—Coffee, the morning paper and a brisk shoeshine under the awnings, across from the shady plaza. Such luxury for so little.

What is the news? Two daughters of Flatnose Lola are in the hands of the *policía*. Same problem mama used to have— peddling Mary J. The narcotic weed can be raised in a window box. A cottage industry.

Flatnose Lola was Dolores Esteván. She was a buster— always in some sort of battle with the Johnny Nabs. The kids have the team spirit.

"They will spend a little time in jail," said the shoeshine man brushing the shoes into mirrors. (In half an hour they will fade to dingy gray. Thus requiring his services again. It is a built-in obsolescence. A secret of Mexican shoeshine men.)

"Ah, but the penitentiaries are not so bad. Movies. Television. Theater. Prisoners do not suffer much these days."

Mexican jails are no Caribbean cruise. But they have improved greatly in the last few years. There are work programs —unlike American prisons where prison labor is not allowed to compete with industry.

Mexican prisoners make Army and institutional clothing. Pay is meager and the Government saves a lot of money.

"There is also the conjugal night," said the shoeshine man. "When the wives of prisoners may visit and stay with their husbands."

He rolled his eyes as if he were describing Sodom and Gomorrah. But a weekly visit of wives to prisoner-husbands is a long established custom in Latin America.

It is also a great incentive to good behavior.

For a lot of co-operation (or maybe enough money to hire a special guard overtime) a prisoner may get a brief shopping trip into town, too.

The Morelos State Prison is in the heart of the red-light district. And in the evening, there is a little parade of prisoners' wives to the gates. Past the gaudy houses (flashes of bright electric light on scarlet hangings). Past the bright saloons (pouring a waterfall of jukebox music into the street).

They carry enameled pans of food on their heads.

A brief taste of home in smoking tortillas and bubbling beans.

There is a men's prison and women's prison. "But separate, of course," said the shoeshine man. "Though in the old days—" He rolled his eyes again.

"The ladies are mostly in prison for shooting—or stabbing. Husbands and sweethearts. The ladies are very nervous. They kill swiftly and regret later.

"The law is understanding about this. In Mexico, we do not punish passion. Much. Just enough so they understand such things cannot be tolerated.

"But women! Woman is a nervous creature. They regret. But what good is that to you if you are dead? If one is married to a nervous woman, one should make a good confession every week. Thus, at least, you escape eternal fire."

"The men," he said, "go to jail for robbery. Man is constructed to be strong and to take what he can. But the ladies go to jail for nervous shooting."

"What makes the Mexican lady so nervous, Maestro?"

"Love," said the shoeshine man. "The more love, the

more nervous. In marriage, a man must be careful the first three years. The years of great love, and clearly, the most dangerous."

Flowers for Breakfast

Cuernavaca—Sunday in Cuernavaca. The sun lies like Aztec gold on the green lawn, on the red-purple masses of bougainvillea. (I wish I could spell that sometime without that nagging doubt.)

It falls gently from the Mexican sky, blue as well-washed blue jeans. At 5000 feet where it is always Spring.

The sun bounces off the broad-leaf mirrors of the banana palms. Softens the lilac spray of the flowering jacaranda trees. Deepens the orange-red flower parasol that tops the lacy flamboyants.

On the far side of the garden are thick patches of what looks like marigolds. The flower of the dead—*flor de muerto*—says Manuel, who gardens this house.

Because in November, on the Day of the Dead, people take them to the cemetery.

There are long stalks of *lirios*. Star-shaped. Big as a butter plate and yellow as the butter.

Little clumps of *Bandera de Mexico*—the flag of Mexico —because of its three colors. The bright green leaf. The white flower. The scarlet pistils clumped in the center.

There is a green parrot in a cage. His name is Lorenzo.

In the center of the garden there is a turquoise swimming pool.

This is Sunday in Cuernavaca. State of Morelos, Mexico. The town where Cortez fought across the dividing, deep barranca against Indians who skinned captive Spaniards and dressed their hides like leather and hung them on pagan altars.

The eyewitness soldier-historian Bernal Diaz wrote:

"We arrived at the large town of Cuernavaca in a very strong situation, on account of the deep ravine which runs at a depth of at least forty feet and the Indians had broken the bridges.

"We at length discovered a dangerous pass over some trees which hung across from the two opposite sides of the ravine. About thirty of us made our way over by the help of these trees. Three fell and one broke his leg.

"It was indeed a truly frightful attempt. I for a time entirely lost my sight from the depth and danger. We who got over fell on the flank and rear of the enemy unexpectedly . . ."

We look across the garden, across the deep ravine (but the trees that bridged it are long gone).

The shaded, broad veranda is paved with great square, red tiles. And pocked-stone Aztec gods look down from niches cut out in the stone wall.

From the town comes the distant clang of iron bells in the fortress cathedral. Built by Cortez in honor of God and his preservation from pagan Indians, which allowed him to bring New Spain into the hands of Charles V and the Holy Roman Empire.

Alongside the shaded plaza is the palace he built. Its back wall is painted with Rivera's murals. Spaniards branding Indian slaves. Spanish armored soldiers crawling across the trees over the barranca.

On Sunday, Indians come from the back country to see them. Dressed in white pajamas of the hot country. Sandals on their feet. Straw hats on their heads. The women plait red cloth into shining black hair that hangs down the back.

There is no monument in Mexico to the conqueror.

Sunday falls in sunlit peace, here in the land of flowers

for breakfast. (In the center of town, there is a political parade. But the loudspeaker orations fade before they come over the brown, folded hills.)

A half-dozen buzzards are floating like gliders on the air currents of the sky. The scavenger birds who clean up the debris of Mexico. (And keep it cleaner than North American highways.)

The morning plane hums down to Acapulco on the Pacific. Where Manila galleons made port with exotic plates from China on the long journey to the tables of Seville.

This is Sunday in Cuernavaca.

The East Coast

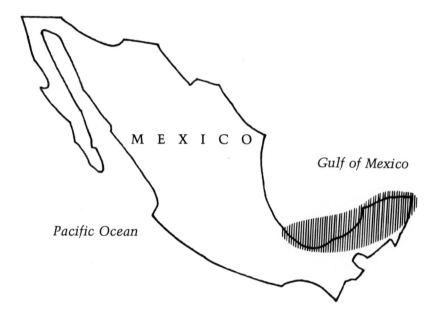

MEXICO

Gulf of Mexico

Pacific Ocean

"The Waikiki" was the biggest, noisiest, raunchiest dance hall in Mexico. Sullen-looking Indian girls sat in foursomes at the tables, waiting to be invited on the floor or to one of the dingy, one-hour rental hotels nearby.

Even so it had a certain jaunty outlook. A sign on the wall said:

"Caballeros: Please do not throw cigarette butts on the floor. The Señoritas are dancing barefoot."

As tourist business became important, the government decided "The Waikiki" was not a good image. So they closed it. Sic transit gloria.

Viva La Revolución!

Veracruz—We drove out of warm Veracruz and began the long climb that takes you to a breathtaking 10,000 feet where you look down on Mexico City. The sweeping panorama Cortez saw as he prepared to attack the Aztec capital: Tenochititlán, the golden city on the silver lakes.

At the top of the pass you are in pine trees. The air is brisk. The sun is warm as a fresh tortilla. The two volcanoes, Popo and the Sleeping Lady, float snowcapped in the blue Mexican sky.

It was the celebration of the Revolution. We passed through villages dressed in flags. Great pinwheels of fireworks stood in the plaza to be fired that night.

Indians in white pajamas were whooping it up at the corner saloon.

Juke boxes fired loud country music into the streets.

Some of the villagers were already staggering. It is no disgrace on holidays to be drunk in these villages. Life is hard enough. They drink a sugar cane alcohol—twice the strength of our whiskey—stepping up the flavor with Coca Cola.

The scenery changes: From Veracruz and coco palms to coffee and vanilla. To pine trees and the blue smokey plumes of the charcoal burners.

We stopped at a roadside stand for a cold, dark beer from Orizaba. An Indian came over.

"Where dost thou go, my friend?"

He put an arm over my shoulder. He looked at me with affection. He blew alcohol fumes in my face.

"To the capital, Señor. Permit me to offer you a drink."

He said: "No, I will buy you a drink. You permit it?"

I permitted it—these people get mad easily. One minute they "thou" you and love you. The next they shift to a formal "Señor." And blow your head off.

I had a tequila—straight. (If you can't lick 'em, join 'em.)

He approved of that. I bought *him* a drink.

"Stay for the fireworks," he said. "Pure blasting powder from the mines. I helped make them."

I said it was a crying shame, but friends waited for me in Mexico City.

He said: "God be with you then. May we meet again."

When I drove off, he was weeping on the bar and reaching for another drink.

We had lunch in Puebla. It's at 7000 feet. The plaza is full of fine old trees. Every wall is flooded with flaming bougainvillea.

The town is getting a seedy look about it. Too many tourists coming through on their way south. ("Poor Mexico!" said President Porfirio Diaz. "So far from God, so near to the United States.")

We had lunch on the plaza. The usual starved looking dogs watched from the sidewalk.

They are a product of survival. They are not *really* starved. They look that way, and the tourists say: "Look at the poor dog." They throw him a cracker.

If the cracker is not buttered, the dog turns it down. What he is really waiting for is a piece of your Serrano ham.

The plaza was full of people. Soft drink stands were doing a roaring business.

Then we drove up to the pass and began the descent into the valley. Only a couple of patches of the great lakes are left. The Spanish drained them. When the great winds blow, dust clouds sweep the city.

Across the Ferry

Veracruz—Veracruz is a tropical seaport town. "The Rich City of the True Cross." Cortez named it. He went up the coast later because of the plague of mosquitoes.

It was the entry point from Spain. Scott's American troops went ashore here in 1847. And the port was known for its summers of yellow fever.

The road from Córdoba enters through a graveyard.

It was Sunday and lively in the little plaza. I bought dark Orizaba beer and a little crab, restuffed with shredded crab meat, raisins and herbs.

A bus driver said the dirt coastal road north to Tecolutla was "very ugly." I should take the highway, the old Cortez route to Jalapa.

It was Sunday, as I said. And on Sunday, the locals go to church. After church they drink *pulque*. And by nightfall the

road is filled with staggering, white-pajamaed Indians. They get good-natured, staggering, blind drunk. It is a traffic hazard.

The road climbs high to the little Indian town of Perote. The Spaniards built a great fort across the road in 1770. During the 1830s, several hundred Texans were imprisoned here after being marched down from El Paso. Many died.

It was high and chilly. The Indians were wrapped in serapes. And on the street corners they sold blocks of crumbly sugar and coconut. A quick shot of energy.

The road to Tecolutla on the coast turns south here. Winding down with clouds lying across the road. Through Indian villages with juke boxes blaring out of *pulque* saloons where one glaring white light hangs from the ceiling.

By the time it turned completely dark I was on the moist coast land. Dodging Indians, burros and buses parked for no particular reason on the road.

I had swung around one bus and then braked just in time. The bus was stopped for the very reason that the road ran right off into water.

I went back and looked at the sign: "Ferry Landing."

There was a small hut with Coca Cola stacked on wooden shelves, and I went in to talk it over. The ferry, said the owner, ran every quarter of an hour.

"Does it run every quarter hour at this time?"

"Ah, who knows? The last one came an hour ago. Have a beer."

There was a litter of pups playing around the fire on the dirt floor. The owner's lady was dressed coolly in bare feet and a ragged dress.

I had beer and some very fresh shrimp with hot sauce and lime juice.

"Where did you learn Spanish?" asked the lady.

"I was a sailor. On the Mexican coast."

"My husband is a sailor. A Yucatán sailor. He was a great man, a fine man. But he left me. Sailors are no good."

"When was that, Señora? Can I have more shrimp?"

"Certainly, Señor. He sailed away ten years ago. I have been sad."

The owner poured me some more beer and smiled philosophically. The lady had several children playing among the empty bottles and was expecting another shortly. It appeared that her sadness had not prevented her acceptance of fate.

"And I used to work in a bar in Veracruz," she added. She launched into a story of life in Veracruz and her husband. The owner said nothing. Obviously, she speaks to him often of the fine life she gave up. And for what?

Fortunately, the quarter-of-an-hour ferry decided to come over and pick up some business. And we all drove aboard. The big tropical moon coming down through a milky sky. And we backed off into the little dirt main street of Tecolutla and got to the hotel on the beach just in time for dinner.

The American Colony

Cuautla—Some people over in Cuautla gave me a splendid welcome party the other day. Corn chips and wonderful refried beans; a magnificent *mole* sauce and rice; mashed avocado juiced with a hot sauce that would blow the vault at Brinks.

They shot off a lot of rockets—it's a very special honor.

Cuautla is an Indian town in the highlands on the road to Veracruz. Some years ago it was discovered by artists and writers—the cost of living was terribly low. Even now it's not bad.

I did a piece on it then and one of the people said reproachfully: "I hope you don't do that again. It was very unfair."

I said: "Do you know, I can't remember *ever* writing about Cuautla. I can't even remember when I was here."

One of the men at the party came by and he said: "Now you've had a look at Cuautla, I think you'll have better perspective than last time."

I said: "I'm sure I will. But I still can't remember the piece."

He said: "Be careful who you talk to. I saw you talking to Joe Mumble. Now Joe has been down here 18 years. And that's the trouble with him. You'd think he'd *invented* Mexico."

He said: "Joe never gets off the golf course. Nice guy, you understand. I think the world of Joe. But he's a big bag of wind."

I said: "I was trying to find out how it is to live down here. I talked to Popsicle and he said—"

The man said: "Popsicle! For the love of—. I mean, you couldn't talk to a worse source than old Pop."

I said: "He said he came here a year ago and liked it."

He said: "That's the trouble with these Johnny-come-latelys. How does he know what he likes when he's only had a year to look it over?"

He went over to the picture windows and he said: "It's going to rain this afternoon."

I said: "How do you know?"

He said: "When you've been here as long as I have, you feel it." He said: "You wouldn't have a drink, would you? I don't want to bend your ear. But I could straighten out a few things these people probably pumped into you."

I said: "Will rum be all right?"

He said: "With a little ice. Now I saw you talking to Artichoke. Great guy, but you could land Art on the moon and he couldn't find earth again with Houston control running the show for him.

"Art's problem is he's on the sauce. I mean there's a man who polishes his liver with pure gin."

He said: "That article you wrote—" I said: "What was in it? I don't remember it at all."

He said: "Well, you said the Cuautla colony was kind of hippie. And they drank too much—. I forget, but it was a knock.

I mean, you bum-rapped us."

He said: "I'll take another as long as you're pouring for yourself. Now I saw Fumble pushing something or other onto you. I *hope* not those paintings—if that's art, I'm for passing a law against it.

"Don't get me wrong. Fumble's OK. *And* he's got beautiful reviews. They all say he's the greatest. I don't know anything about art, but I know what I like."

He said: "I've got nothing against you personally, understand? But how you ever got that article out! Were you drunk? I've got nothing against a man who drinks. Like a nip myself now and then."

I said: "To tell you the truth, I don't remember a single thing about that column."

He said: "Well, you probably *were* drunk then. Nothing against you. We've all got our weak spots. I could tell you—. But maybe I'd better not. Anyway, cheers!"

And Thus We Set Out

Jalapa—Every conqueror of Mexico has struggled up the rugged cordillera, from steamy Veracruz to the thin air of Mexico City.

"In compliance with our requisition, fifty of the principal Tononacan warriors attended us and also 200 men to draw our guns. And thus we set out from Cempoal in the month of August, 1519, our army in good order and patrols of cavalry and light infantry in front. Our first day's march was to a town named Jalapa."

So begins the great eye-witness account of the Conquest by the soldier Bernal Diaz del Castillo.

The sun and warm weather had come back to Mexico. It was a spring day at Jalapa, a two-hour drive from Veracruz, but already more than 4000 feet above sea level. Across the staggering peaks and barrancas, you could see the great snowy peak of Orizaba in the blue Mexican sky.

The new road follows, intersects and cuts around the old cobbled, guttered road the Spanish used for three centuries. It is loaded with history.

At Cerro Gordo on April 12, 1847, Scott's Regulars drove off the Mexican lancers of Santa Ana.

Off the road above Jalapa is the town of Venta de Lencero, a spire of the church tower rising above the village. Diaz remembers a fellow soldier of the Conquest:

"Lencero, a good soldier, had an inn on the road to Vera Cruz.

At 8000 feet, I stopped for gas at Perote where they sell a sugary candy. Across the town is the squat stone fortress of San Carlos de Perote. Several hundred Texan prisoners spent a miserable two years in the cells.

When the fort surrendered to Scott's advance elements, the Mexican commander took a receipt from a Captain of Engineers, Robert E. Lee.

Somewhere beyond here in the Tlascalan mountains, the westbound Spanish conquistadors grew faint-hearted. Four snow-capped volcanoes are in sight and the pine hills jump straight up from the sandy plains covered with spiked blue-green *maguey* plants.

A number of the soldiers wanted to return to Veracruz. Said Cortez;

"It is better instead of repining to look forward and leave all to be guided by the hand of God.

"As to our return, it is true that the natives we have left behind are now friendly. But if we seemed to retreat, the very stones would rise against us.

"Therefore, gentlemen, thus it is: Bad there, worse elsewhere. Better stay as you are, here in a plentiful country; and as to what you say of losses, deaths and fatigues, such is the fortune of war, and we did not come here in search of pastimes and amusements."

The Mexican highlands are majestic in the sunlight. One of Scott's officers wrote home: "The soldiers marched often in silence, awed by their surroundings."

The roads are full of buses. Bus travel is cheap and plentiful in Mexico now. Thirty years ago, the Indians seldom got more than ten miles from their villages. Now they pack into the buses and go booming down the highways.

The bicycle is also making inroads on Mexico. You cannot ride a bicycle on village cobbles. But you can walk it to the highway and take off.

And on a warm afternoon, I drove over the pass into the Valley of Mexico. Flat, filled with traffic, and every plaza full of business and music. Once it held two great lakes around the Aztec city. But now it is drained, salt-edged. The winds blow dust clouds. It must have been magnificent when Bernal Diaz topped the pass and remembered in his journal:

"When I behold the scenes that were around me, I thought within myself that this was the garden of the world. But all is destroyed and that which was a lake is now a field of corn, and so altered that the natives themselves would hardly know it."

Maya Country

Mérida—Mérida is an old colonial city, dating back to twenty years after the Conquest. Narrow, cobbled streets. A bustling big market full of strange tropical fruits and bright cloth. Handmade tin pots. Stoves tinsmithed from 5-gallon gasoline cans.

In a corner of the market, I found two vintage Victrolas. The kind wound by hand, with a big, ornate horn speaker on top. A handful of old records to go with them.

This is Maya country. I had lunch with a man from Mérida who said: "Three-fourths of the people in the back country only speak Maya. No Spanish at all.

"In Yucatán, we are so different from the rest of Mexico

we don't think of ourselves as Mexican. We are *Yucateños*.

"Are you interested in Mayan ruins? I don't mean the tourist places that have been cleaned up. Like Uxmal and Chichén Itzá. I mean ruins in the deep jungles. "In Quintana Roo, there's an Indian village. And only a day's walk from there—. No. I didn't go. But someday—. It's a whole Mayan city, they said. Nobody—no white man—has seen it."

He said: "I hear some fellow—the Kon Tiki man?—built a boat of papyrus. Like the Egyptians made in ancient times. He wanted to see if he could sail to Yucatán to prove the Mayans came from Egypt. Or from the lost Atlantis.

"Maybe it's true. There's a relief in stone on the wall at Chichén Itzá that shows a boat very similar. Who knows?"

Mérida is a clean, tropical town. It is named for Mérida in Spain. The Amérida of the Romans where the Roman forum and the Roman theater are finer than anything in Rome.

The men wear the white *guaybera*. It's a coat-like shirt with a rather military cut.

The market is full of fine Panama hats, woven from a Yucatán palm.

There is a great shady plaza. A bustling place. Soft drink stands. An army of shoeshine boys. There's nothing so restful as sitting in a shaded plaza while your shoes are shined.

The seafood is excellent. Specials are *huachinango*—red

snapper—and baby shark. Conch soup is superb.

Because it was on the menu and I *had* to find out what it was, I ordered "poor gentlemen." It turned out to be bread pudding with raisins. Just like grandma used to make.

Not many tourists get down this way. The service is better. The hotels give you the correct exchange. (In tourist Mexico, the hotels take a big bite when they move dollars into pesos. The same when they change them back.)

The man from Mérida said: "The music is better in Yucatán, too. More sad and plaintive than up in Mexico."

The little orchestra struck up *"Caminante del Mayab"*— a sad song of the Mayans.

It reminded me I had a request from a daughter: "Bring back a guitar."

I said: "If you think I'm going to pack a guitar all over Mexico, you're out of your mind."

But now after lunch—well, beer and red snapper mellows a man.

The man from Mérida said: "The guitars here are excellent. If you don't have time to go to a shop, let's send a waiter."

We gave a waiter $28 for a guitar, $2 for a taxi. He had it back in half an hour. "A magnificent guitar," said the man from Mérida. I got on the plane loaded with a guitar. Scratching my ankles. Full of beer and red snapper. And happy, don't forget that.

The Deep Blue Sea

Cozumel—A damp warm morning on the island of Cozumel. The fishing and scuba diving boats are going out. Cutting a white path through a lead-to-silver sea under grey clouded skies.

There's a mist of rain. A tropical rain smell in the air. The flame trees are showers of Chinese red blossoms. Big creped-red hibiscus everywhere—but the chunky little brown Mayan maids never wear them.

The waiter brings steaming high-roast Mexican coffee beside the sea and assures me this is *not* the rainy season.

"September, Señor, is when it rains." (Not so. Now, in May, is when the rains come.)

This is an Aeromexico flight. From dry Tijuana in Baja

California to the wet jungles of Yucatán. A long 3400-mile diagonal across Mexico.

It's the land of the Mayas. *Chac* is the rain god here. *Tlaloc* controls umbrella weather up in Aztec Mexico City.

The country is full of great, silent Mayan cities fallen to ruin. They are being looted shamefully.

In the state capital, Mérida, they told me: "We have more than 300 *known* archeological sites. We cannot police them all."

Several hundred may have never been dug into. Police collared a gang who were stealing an entire Mayan temple.

They had sawed the façade into portable blocks that could be stuck together again.

The Mérida man said: "They even had night lights so they could work 24 hours. Where would they sell it? Clearly they had an order from somebody. Who could afford such a thing except some rich man in North America?"

Collecting pre-Columbian art is a big thing now. It's all bootlegged—against the law to take it out of the country.

The Mérida man said: "They caught these. How many others are there they didn't catch? Everywhere you go in the back country there are Indians who can take you to Mayan ruins that have never been put on the maps."

Less than ten years ago, Cozumel was a native fishermen's island. Juan de Grijalra charted it on an early voyage. Cortez saw it from his ships as he sailed to the Conquest.

Now there are daily jet flights. A half dozen hotels.

You can rent scuba gear. A jeep. A red Honda motorcycle. A killer. Unpaved Cozumel already has a traffic fatality score.

The waiter said: "Already this year 16 killed on the Honda and 200 wounded."

He said it proudly. It shows Cozumel is coming right up with the rest of the modern, murdering world.

A girl in a bikini came in to breakfast, skinned from knee to stern. Her Honda hit sand and—Dear John, that's all she wrote.

The man in Mérida said: "They not only rob the jungle ruins, the tourists take pieces from the walls at well-known places like Chichén Itzá."

This old Mayan capital is the most famous of the ruins.

You drive out in a couple of hours from Mérida. There's

a hotel. The ruins have been cleared—great impressive pyra-mids and temples.

The Mérida man said: "In the museum at the entrance, they had three carved jaguars. Three sizes. Like the mama, the papa and the little one.

"Well, somebody came along and just put the little one under his arm and walked out! I tell you some people are bandits at heart!"

I said: "What do you think they do with them? Do they sell them?" He said: "No, there is plenty to be stolen by commercial thieves in the unexplored ruins.

"I think this was just a tourist. He takes the little jaguar home. He says to his friends: 'Look at this nice little souvenir I got at the ruins.'"

Of course if the Mexican police catch you, they put you away until you are good and sorry.

What's Doing Lately

Cozumel—You know you're in Mexico when:

You stub your toe on that unexpected step-up into the bathroom.

You pinch your thumb between the door knob and the

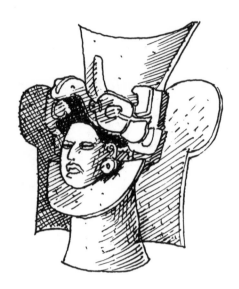

door jamb. (How do they engineer them so carefully for this?)

Woke this blue Caribbean morning with pinched thumb and stubbed toe. "Mexico is a true Paradise," said the tourist bureau folder. "Of all the lands in Paradise, none is more lovely than the island of Cozumel."

The electricity was off in Paradise, and the hot water had gone off duty. But this is the warm tropics. We shave in the cold water.

Wrote a postcard to my boy: "The pirates didn't cry when *they* had to shave in cold water." (Of course the pirates were full of rum.)

Cozumel is an emerald jewel island. Coco palms lean against the wind. Low jungle hides ancient Mayan ruins at the far end.

There is a little town, San Miguel de Cozumel. A rather bare plaza. A clock tower on the municipal building—the clock stopped at five after one. The town closes down at one in the afternoon.

A lone dog was ranging the plaza, and a boy went by on a red scooter. *Put-put-put.*

A couple of fishing boats rolled on the edge of the turquoise sea. You can look across the water and see the green shores of mainland Quintana Roo, twelve miles away.

The Restaurant Chichén Itzá was open. It is open-air under a thatch roof. In the back they have a scooter rental station. While I was having Yucatecan beer, the waiter went back and wheeled a scooter through the dining room for a customer on the sidewalk.

I said: "Could I have a *ceviche de caracol*?"

"Immediately, Señor." (They make a good *ceviche* of conch. Chop it in chunks. Marinate it raw in lime juice for an hour. Serve it covered with chopped onions, chopped hot peppers, salt and more lime juice.)

He came back with the *ceviche* in one hand and a gasoline can in the other. Gave me the *ceviche*. Went out and filled the scooter tank.

It's a relaxed life around Restaurant Chichén Itzá.

"Cozumel was frequented by pirates," says the tourist folder. "Among them were Lafitte and Henry Morgan."

Cozumel lies off the great bump that Yucatán puts into the Caribbean. It was a landfall for early navigators running from the rum-and-sugar islands to the feverish ports of Mexico.

The deep azure waters are stiff with early shipwrecks. It's great hunting grounds for scuba divers. Fishermen go wild over their catches. And a day's sport is to take a boat, a guide and a lot of beer and ice and go picnicking on a white sand beach.

As you go, you fish. The cook-guide cuts some of the catch up and marinates it for *ceviche*. You can pull in red

snapper—*huachinango*—as fast as you can bait and throw out the line.

When you land, he builds a driftwood fire. And while you eat your *ceviche*, the fish is being grilled for the second course.

The waiter sat down with me. He said: "Where do you stay?" "*Cabañas del Caribe.*" "How much do you pay?"

When I told him, he said: "Too much. Stay next door at the Hotel Lopez. Eat here. We have an international cuisine."

He brought me the menu. It was extensive, and somebody had done an English translation. "Fruit Juice" came out "Juicy Fruits."

"Could I have some of the crab?" I said.

"Well," he said, "we're all out of that today. In fact, we're all out of fish. The fisherman didn't come today because his wife is sick.

"But ordinarily," he said, "we have a magnificent dinner. But today the chef didn't come either. *Mañana*—"

Baja California

M E X I C O

Gulf of Mexico

Pacific Ocean

In the late Sunday afternoon, the village Indians in white cotton pajama suits stagger homeward down the middle of the road, each supported by a stocky wife.

"In Mexico no one is arrested for being drunk," said a Mexican judge. "There are charges: 'Drunk and insulting the police.' 'Drunk and fighting with the police.' 'Drunk and making a scandal.' But there is no charge of being plain drunk.

"The country Mexican works hard all week. On Sunday morning he goes to Mass. In the afternoon he drinks in a bar. To arrest him for being drunk would deny him his dignity and his civil rights."

Blow the Man Down

La Paz—A warm and sunny day on the Sea of Cortez. A few ragged palms along the beach. Copper-colored hills behind the town of La Paz.

The sparkling white *Island Princess* is anchored in a blue bay and ship's launches chug back and forth to the shore.

We are exploring cruise ports in the Gulf of California. Local people marvel at a ship of this size—581 passengers and a crew of 320. When we hit the beaches, it's an invasion.

I got a taxi on the shore and headed for town. The taxi driver said: "How many people on that enormous boat, Señor?"

I said: "Altogether, about 900."

"God save us," said the taxi driver. "La Paz will lie in ruins."

Sports fishermen have discovered Baja California. La Paz is a bustling town.

There are several small—but good—tourist hotels. A new Presidente has been built and the older Los Arcos has added a wing. Expensive fishing boats rock on the quiet bay. And at one store, you can buy the day's Los Angeles newspapers.

Even so, 900 ship's visitors is a shock.

It's a brown land. The desert comes down to the edge of the ink-blue water. Cactus and mesquite.

Great Cortez himself came here after the Conquest. He marched around the beach, moving stones and making sword cuts in scruffy trees. All noted by the Royal Notary.

He took over the land for Charles of Spain. Left a small colony—which went broke immediately.

Later expeditions found the sea crammed with oysters. And for years, they flooded Spain with pearls.

A sleepy Mexican colonial village at the end of nowhere. La Paz escaped revolutions. Survived William Walker, soldier-of-fortune—"the grey-eyed man of destiny."

It sold beans to Baja cowboys. Fished for shrimps. Dozed in summer heat.

Then the sports fishermen came—the Sea of Cortez is stuffed with marlin and grouper. Rooster fish and dorado. Sailfish that go 150 pounds.

Now come the big cruise ships. Soon we'll be saying: "Why, I remember La Paz when—."

The taxi driver said: "If these big ships come all the time, Señor, we will soon be rich. Like Acapulco. Like Puerto Vallarta."

He said: "*Dios*, if I were rich, I would buy five more taxis."

He said: "You know Luis Coppola? He owns the Hotel Los Arcos."

He said: "You see the new building he adds to the hotel? You see the new Presidente hotel?"

"Believe me, Señor, when you see those people building and building, then you know those rich people are going to get richer.

"What a pity that I have no money. Ah, thank you, Señor, you are generous. Good journey to you. God travel with you."

Morning Full of Birdsong

La Paz—In the warm Baja California dawn, a bunch of birds got up and held a noisy convention outside my window. The sun was just coming up from mainland Mexico. The Sea of Cortez turned Aztec gold.

Somewhere back of town a dozen roosters bugled challenges to the world.

An early motorcycle rider went pop-popping along the bay road. Demonstrating morning machismo—the strutting maleness Mexicans love so well.

The taxi drivers began washing their cars on the street below. They shouted back and forth the news of last night's conquests. Mexico gets up early. No use trying to sleep through it. I got up and shaved—a dull blade.

(What is this in the morning mirror? The man in the Sta-Prest shirt with the Sta-Prest face. Wash them in Lux. The creases return magically.)

We flew up from Cabo San Lucas to La Paz on a panting DC-3. The strip on the tip of Baja is dirt. You take off through a desert land of dry mesquite and cactus, edging the blue Pacific northward.

A handful of passengers. A hotel man and his young son. Four sullen looking Indian girls sat playing cards.

They've been operating a branch of a La Paz bordello on the cape during the sports fishing season.

They looked like business had been disappointing. Or they had hangovers. Maybe both.

I checked into the Hotel Los Arcos and immediately fell over the bathroom step.

For some reason, Mexico makes all bathrooms with a step up or a step down—I forget that. It is a tourist hazard. Mexican doctors are always putting casts on tourists who fall over the step.

Another tripper is the doorknob. Mexican builders engineer the doorknob so that it pinches your fingers when you close it. The trick is to stand back. Give the doorknob a sharp pull to get the door going. Then *jerk* your hand out of the way.

La Paz is the Big Town—a sports fishing town. From here to mainland Mexico, the Sea of Cortez is loaded with fish.

Marlin. Sailfish. Grouper. Dorado. A dozen luxury fishing boats are rocking on the bay. Los Arcos is full of fishermen.

It's the older hotel now—the new hotels have been built on the beach some three miles out of town. But Los Arcos is modernized and has charm.

A patio full of blazing bougainvillea. The front veranda has a line of old-fashioned rocking chairs. At night, you can sit looking over the warm bay. A big slice of golden papaya moon rises over the black water. The beer is cold. And the dust of Mexico—(you will find peace in no other land)—has settled on your heart.

St. Joseph Comes Marching In

La Paz—We went to José's turtle birthday party the other day, and it's certainly worth some social notes.

It was the feast day of San José—St. Joseph. In Latin America you don't celebrate your birthday which after all, is only a gloomy reminder that it's later than you thought.

Instead you celebrate your saint's day. All over Mexico, Josés were being congratulated. Since there are lots of Josés, it was as though all the Smiths in the U.S. had

birthday parties on the same day.

Even the towns—there are many San José of Something—hold celebrations. Down at the tip of Baja, the town of San José del Cabo got ready for an all-out bust.

The taxi driver said: "Everybody will get drunk, drunk, *drunk.*"

José is a general handyman at Hotel La Posada in La Paz. In his sturdy 60's, I'd guess. He asked me to his party when he carried the bags in.

At six in the gray morning, José got up and built a mesquite fire under the palms in back of the hotel. Then he began to cook the sea turtle. I took down the recipe—in case you want to do this at home.

Get a 50 kilo sea turtle. (A kilo is 2.2 pounds.) You take off the breast shell with the meat attached and prop it against two sticks facing the fire. This slow roast goes on for five hours.

Two hours before the *cahuama*—(local for sea turtle)—is done, you make a stew in a 20-quart pot. Tomatoes, onions, green chiles, peas, oregano and red wine.

The roasted meat is then scraped from the shell. Some of it is put in the stew. Some goes into the dish-like top shell which goes on the coals to keep warm. Serves 80.

Happy Saint's Day, Don José!

All his friends came to José's party. All the maids and all the waiters. The bartender came leaving a junior assistant at the bar. All the taxi drivers who hang around La Posada came.

Bill Callahan, the owner, came. I came. Papagayo Al Williams, the Mexican restaurant man from San Francisco, was already there.

Everybody brought beer and wine and whiskey.

They embraced José: "Congratulations, José."

They stood around and drank a *lot* of whiskey. José drank with all of them.

The *cahuama* steamed fragrantly in the shell. We picked out pieces of delicious liver, folded them in hot tortillas and ate them with green *jalapeño* peppers that could blow a safe.

Two sets of guitar players showed up. They took turns playing and eating and drinking.

They played happy songs and everybody laughed. They played sad songs and everybody wept. It was a saintly day.

At four o'clock I gave José the hugging *abrazo* of Mexico. I said: "Don José, two thousand thanks. Congratulations again."

At six o'clock there was a lot of guitar music under my window. The waiters were wheeling José down the path in a deck chair. And while the guitars played, they tossed him in the swimming pool.

Very few waiters showed up for breakfast this morning. The ones who came looked hung over.

The Evening Sun Goes Down

La Paz—We sit outside on the patio at La Posada and watch the sun go down. The sun goes down behind us. Beyond the desert hills over the Pacific. But it leaves a blue and gold pattern on the Sea of Cortez.

There was just enough chill in the air to burn a mesquite fire. It's a scrubby desert brush—this is thorny country. Everything that grows is ready to stab you.

The cowboys in Baja California wear huge chaps, a quarter-inch thick cowhide. The cattle are scrawny. They work hard for a living.

It's not an easy country. The Jesuit missionaries were hard put to get enough to live on. The few thin Indians had ways of recycling cactus fruit you wouldn't believe.

A pleasant evening as the sun goes down. *Que lástima*, I have to go. Away from the fishing boats rocking on the sunstruck blue water. Away from the brown desert, the tall *cirio* cactus and the eagles wheeling overhead.

Away from the diving brown pelicans and the sailing frigate birds. The porpoises leaping in great gunmetal curves. The shrimp boats where we buy a fresh kilo for a few dollars, boil them on the boat and peel them to go with cold beer.

I said to Bill Callahan who runs La Posada: "I don't think I'll go. I think I'll stay here and open a taco stand."

It's a weepy evening in La Paz.

The new 1000-mile highway opens the primitive country. (You could do worse than opening a taco stand. Maybe a chain. Maybe a McDonald's—we'll ruin the country yet.)

There weren't many Mexican handicrafts in Baja. Where they had them—baskets, saddle making—the government has built little market stalls on the highway.

All of them were empty. So at Miraflores—where they made chaps and saddles—I drove three miles off the highway to the village.

It's a pretty little town. Flowery tulip trees on the dusty main street. A small monument to "the mothers" at the end. A number of falling-down, deserted houses that must have been grand in their day.

The saddle maker worked under a thatched roof beside a garden full of fruit trees and flowers.

He said: "There is nothing to sell because we have no cowhide."

I said: "Man, there *must* be cowhide in Baja. What did you do before?"

He said vaguely that once there was cowhide. "Now there is none."

At the basket town they said: "There are no mate-

rials to make the baskets." I said: "What did you used to do?"

They said: "There was material. Now there isn't any."

In La Paz, a man told me: "You know how it is in Mexico. A village sells some handicraft. In the markets. To other villages.

"Then one day a trader comes from Mexico City. He says: 'These are good baskets. I want to buy a thousand of them.'

"Immediately the basket maker is overwhelmed. He thinks: 'If I have to make a thousand baskets, I will have no time for the fiestas. I will have no time for the cantina.' He is so shook up he stops making *any* baskets."

There are several tourist stores in La Paz. They sell things brought from the mainland. Taxco silver. Saltillo serapes. Straw hats from Morelia.

The prices are higher than what they charge the tourists in the Pink Zone in Mexico City.

With Water on the Side

Cabo San Lucas—At six in the warm Mexican morning we came around the rocky tip of Baja California. The sun was just coming up—a coin of Aztec gold over the blue Sea of Cortez.

The *Island Princess*, gleaming white in the early sun-light, came into the bay dead slow. The water swelled like blown green glass. The air smelled of salt water and wet, newly washed decks.

The little brown town of Cabo San Lucas lay asleep beside the white sand beach and a forked-tail frigate bird sailed in a sky of washed blue-jean denim. A Mexican Immigration boat headed for us piling up a sugary bow wave.

The room phone rang:"This is the Purser's Office. Please report here to clear Immigration."

I said:"I'm still in pajamas, man! I haven't had coffee."

The phone said:"As soon as possible." Click.

Princess Cruises was bought in 1974 by British P and O Line. It's not easy to find new cruise ports. The *Island Princess* started exploring the Sea of Cortez, 400 miles of blue water gulf between the Baja peninsula and mainland Mexico.

There was a great screaming of wire falls as the ship's launches went down to the water.

The phone rang again. I came dripping out of the shower: "Immigration has gone back to shore. He didn't bring the right rubber stamps. You can go back to bed."

I said:"Back to bed? Are you out of your mind?"

But the phone only went quietly—click.

It was a crazy idea anyway. I thought I'd get off at San

Lucas—air taxi to La Paz and meet the *Princess* there the next day. There are 581 passengers on the ship. I was the only one who needed a special rubber stamp.

The launches began ferrying passengers to the shore. San Lucas is three blocks of dusty main street. One curio store. Resort hotels that might give lunch to a hundred people in a pinch.

The phone rang and said: "You must go ashore to collect your tourist card from Immigration."

There is only one Immigration officer in San Lucas. (Who needs more?) A girl in the next office said: "He has gone back to the ship."

I went up the hill by taxi to Hotel Finisterra. Got out on the breezy deck and ordered a cold XXX beer. I squeezed some lemon in the rim of the can and salted it.

The manager came up and said: "La Paz radio says your plane will be here at 1:45."

I took a launch back to the ship. They said: "The Immigration officer has gone back to his office with your tourist cards."

I launched back. The girl said: "He is looking for you. He went back to the ship."

I taxied back to the Finisterra—there are no phones in San Lucas. I said: "Radio and cancel that plane." The manager said: "We cannot get any reception on the radio."

I told the manager to keep on the air. I told him to radio La Paz not to hold my hotel rooms.

I went back on the deck. The last launch came in. The Immigration officer handed me the stamped tourist cards. "There you are, Señor. Now you can go to La Paz."

I went back to the ship—all air-conditioned—took off my shoes and had a big, cold *piña colada*. And it was wonderful, just wonderful.

End of the World

Cabo San Lucas—It's warm here now at the tip of Baja California. The end of the world. From here there's only blue water for 2000 miles to French Polynesia and the Islands-Under-the-Wind.

At the end of the world, there are four luxury hotels

spread across the 20 miles of the cape. The Hotel Finisterra, where I'm staying, is built dramatically into the face of a chalk-brown cliff, a couple of hundred feet above a white sand beach.

Warm days and cold beer. I took off my shoes and threw them in the closet. I sat up in the breezy open bar and had a can of Three X's. You squeeze a little lemon juice into the lip of the can. Salt it. Drink the beer.

"*Qué tal, Señor*. Welcome back to Finisterra. The usual?"

It sounds a little lush when the bartender remembers what you had two years ago. But it's a plus.

The regulars who have found this end of the world are an odd bunch. A famous European chef comes here for three months at a time.

He is built like a wrestler. Has a bullet head and a mid-Europe accent. You could cast him as a German general in "Hogan's Heroes."

He sits in the sun and drinks martinis on the rocks.

The manager said: "Too bad Mr. Kaiser Watanabe isn't here. He flies from Japan four times a year."

Mr. Watanabe became wealthy making paper coffins. I gather they are something like an egg carton. Handsomely done. The family seal embossed on the top.

The manager said: "He explained it one night here—who ever heard of paper coffins? Somebody said: 'Aren't they rather light?' Watanabe said: "I also sell sandbags—one dollar a bag.' "

He said: "Watanabe flies all the way from Tokyo, but he is very careful with his money. He won't hire a fishing boat—no way. He fishes from the pier and from the rocks.

"Then he brings the fish up here and slices them into *sashimi*."

When I tossed my shoes into the closet, my watch stopped. A stem came loose. It can't be wound. Who cares what time it is?

There are no newspapers at the cape. No TV. I can't raise anything on the car radio. We can call the airport at La Paz by radio phone. But we can't telephone a hotel a mile away to see what's on tonight's menu.

In the rose-and-gold evening, the sports fishing boats come in flying victory pennants of the catch. You can read the pennants and see what they've caught. A flag for marlin. A flag for sailfish. A flag for dolphin, the *mahimahi* of Hawaii.

Velvet night falls on the rolling Pacific. In the open bar, high above the beach, a mesquite fire is blazing in a fireplace chopped into the cliff.

The guitar players run their hands over the strings. A shower of golden notes rises to a sky full of stars.

There's supposed to be buried treasure on the beach. A couple of holes where people have dug.

A Baja girl lives up the road. Of such beauty that she can only visit the hotel with a convoy of ferocious aunts. A family treasure.

"Her father sleeps with a shotgun by his bed," said the bartender.

The American fishermen agree that she's a gorgeous muffin. They call her The Incredible Edible.

"Almost had him boated and he broke the line."

The fish stories begin on the second margarita.

"There have always been fish at Baja," said the Mexican boat skipper. "There will *always* be fish at Baja. When God put the people in the Baja desert, He felt sorry for them. So He gave them the fish."

A Pretty Kettle of Fish

Cabo San Lucas—The boat radio spoke up: "*Yo-Yo Two*, this is the *Mariana*. Do you have anything?" *Yo-Yo Two* said: "I can see marlin all over the place. But we can't get a strike."

The Mexican boat captain nudged me: "Look!" Ten black triangular fish tails stood above the water. Marlin! These are the fish that go a hundred pounds. He turned the boat slowly and trailed our two lines by them. Two fat live mackerel on the ends.

Nothing. *"No quieren comer,"* he said. "They just don't want to eat."

The *Suzie E.* rocked gently on the blue Mexican water. Warm sun. Barefoot. I got a cold Tres XXX beer from the refrigerator.

I don't care whether the marlin bite or not. I'm fishing for the good life.

For three days I sat around the elegant Hotel Finisterra listening to fish stories: "Now if you use a 20-pound test line—" ". . . had the leader wrapped around his tail so I—"

Everybody said: "You *must* fish."

We are at the warm end of Baja, California. Remote. No telephones. Days are a sunny 75 degrees. At night a big fat moon comes up from mainland Mexico, and the water turns to melted silver.

The *Suzie E.* is a luxury fishing cruiser. Two bedrooms. One bath. Refrigerator. Lounge cabin. Cassette music comes from the speakers.

Comfortable chairs and an awning on the flying bridge. We also took along a Señorita—to see what happens when 110-pound Girl meets 110-pound Marlin.

The sea was simply full of fish. A couple of dozen seal-brown porpoises began leaping clear of the water alongside. We sighted marlin tails every few minutes.

I must say that fishing this way is pretty easy. The helper hooks a couple of live mackerel on the ends of two rods. He sets the rods in holders. When a fish strikes, he calls you. You sit in a chair and reel it in.

I said: "I'll take photographs. Let the Señorita catch the fish."

Within five minutes *two* dorados hit both lines. About forty pounds each. (This is the eating fish the Hawaiians call *mahimahi.*)

The Señorita pulled one in—no easy job. Then they handed her the other rod, and she reeled that in.

She said: "This is hard work. Wouldn't you like to fish?"

I said, "I'm busy with the camera." I got another beer and slacked off in a boat chair in the shade.

While marlin wouldn't bite, we got a 20-pound yellow tail. And then—bang!

"Sailfish!" the boat captain yelled. He began backing up the *Suzie E.* "Reel in! Reel in!" he shouted. The sailfish came three feet out of the water and tried to shake the hook loose.

The Señorita reeled like crazy. She was dripping wet in the hot sun.

I got another beer. I said: "You know, I'm beginning to *like* fishing."

We towed the sailfish down to the scales—112 pounds. The battle lasted half an hour—and two cold beers.

The Señorita was all worn out. I was fresh as a daisy.

I joined the fish stories last night: "Then the sailfish came out of the water and I—" High times and tequila flowing around Baja California.

Spanish Waters

Cabo San Lucas—At dawn the sea is rose and gray. The sun comes up over the Sea of Cortez. The water turns ink-blue. Sparkling with instant diamonds.

Just off the cape of Baja California, a pair of whales are cruising north to the breeding grounds at Scammon's Lagoon.

The sports fishing boats are putting out to sea where the 100-pound striped marlin are. They stay on top of the water. You can see the black triangle tails—sometimes ten or fifteen at a time.

The weather is warm. The Mexican beer is cold. Barefoot and lazy, that's me. The blue Pacific beats on a hundred miles of white sand beach.

"*Spanish waters, Spanish waters, you are ringing in my ears . . .*"

Fernando is the chief honcho of the little village. Maybe 500 or 600 people. A small fish canning factory supports it.

Fernando has the hotel's sports fishing boats. He owns the little handicraft shop. He seems to have a hand in the taxis—I think there are three.

He can get you a rented horse. Or a box lunch. Or a ride home in the empty seat of a private plane. This final end of the peninsula is on its way to sudden wealth—four luxury hotels already.

Fernando no doubt will be a rich man. *Si, Señor.*

Fernando said: "In the '30s, Señor, there was a lot of money. People fished for sharks. The U.S. bought a lot of shark livers for oil.

"Then I don't know what happened. Maybe depression. Once I heard an old man say he could remember when there was no money in Baja. No money at all. People traded things."

He said: "We are far from Mexico. Mexico City doesn't pay attention to Baja. So we don't *feel* like Mexicans. We feel we are Californians."

Fishermen knew about it. There was one good hotel. Not many other people discovered it.

The climate is magnificent in March. The desert comes right down to the sea in Baja. Dry desert air blows through your room. Washed socks dry in an hour.

No smog. No smoke. Mile after mile of empty, white sand beach. All the peninsula—800 miles of primitive land length—was waiting for the American cities to explode into it.

Fernando said: "Now Mexico City is beginning to look at us. Former President Miguel Alemán bought a lot of land on the cape. A rich American bought all that palm-tree land where the mission used to be."

(That's Robert Maheu, the management man who fought with Howard Hughes' interests in Las Vegas.)

A new Mexican law lets foreigners *own* coastal land. If they are using it for tourist purposes. The old law didn't let you own land within 30 miles of the coast.

This opens Cabo San Lucas to the Hiltons, the Marriotts, the Holiday Inns.

The road is now paved from Ensenada all the way down. And good times are a-coming to Cabo. (The hell with progress, says I. But nobody listens.)

There's a brisk new prosperity in San José del Cabo. (The *big* town—2800 people.) A bright drugstore. It's stocked with the signs of good times: Perfumes. Face lotions. Gay sun hats.

Fishermen are spenders. Hotels here are luxury hotels. The rooms are large. Well furnished. Breezy. With fish coming in daily, the seafood is excellent.

I said: "Fernando, I may never go home." He said: "*Si, Señor.* I know of a house—" Fernando can get you anything.

The West Coast

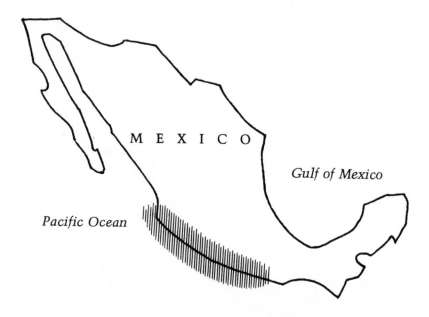

MEXICO

Gulf of Mexico

Pacific Ocean

In the corner of the main plaza of Acapulco, there was a wonderful woman who made wonderful little enchiladas. About the size of your finger.

I wrote about them and I must have written it well.

About a year later, a friend of mine went in to buy some.

"Ah, we don't make those anymore, Señora," said the woman. "Too many people asked for them."

Don't Forget to Write

Bahía San Carlos—After five days at sea, friendships become strong as a wire splice:"Whenever you're in Pomona, be sure to phone!"

(They dwindle off to a Christmas card: "We ought to send a card to Whatsisname. You know. The ones we met on the ship." But in the two weeks of cruising, new friends are warming. We look forward to seeing them each dawning day.)

In the sunstruck afternoon, the *Island Princess* dropped anchor in blue Bahía San Carlos and a Mexican real estate man waited for us on the shore.

The Bay of San Carlos is on the edge of the Sonora desert. The cactus and the tough gray-green mesquite march down to the water's edge. The hills are dry and brown and wind-scarred rocks mark the boundaries of the bay.

The ship's launches chugged in—there's a tourist hotel and a fine white sand beach.

The real estate man ran up and down, offering to show condominiums that begin at $19,000. "Next year they will be worth $25,000!"

The highway runs a few miles from the bay to bustling little Guaymas. But you couldn't get me there with a warrant. From April to November it's hot as a Sheriff's pistol.

Behind the coast highway—twenty or thirty miles—there's a rocky, dirt-tracked road that was once *El Camino Real.* The Royal Highway.

Father Kino, the industrious Jesuit, walked along it, founding stone-and-adobe fortress churches. Preaching the Holy Word to wild, marveling Indians.

The explorer Coronado came through the land, swords sharpened and spurs-a-jingle. The rich Seven Cities of Cibola lay somewhere over the northern horizon. His soldiers cursed the heat and dreamed of gold and cool patios in Spain.

The inland towns are quiet, lost places now. You reach them on bumpy dirt roads: Ures, where the Jesuit order had headquarters for northern Mexico.

Arizpe—it was once the frontier capital for all Spanish lands from here to Canada. De Anza who founded San Francisco is buried in the church.

Alamos. Once it was so rich that a mine owner paved the path from his home to the church with silver bricks.

There are legends of lost mines. Plunder from the revolution. Indian ghosts and Yaqui loot.

The real estate man was full of enthusiasm:"We expect—without doubt, Señor—that Bahía San Carlos will be more popular than Acapulco!"

Some years ago I stayed at the hotel—B.C. (Before Condominiums.) I tried to buy some land—it was terribly cheap. Immediately the owner jumped the price five times.

He was amazed that anyone wanted the land at all. But if they did, he intended to charge all he could. (I've been thankful ever since that I didn't get it.)

I think I made the first offer. The Father of Bahía San Carlos.

Sunset is the best time in the desert. We got back on the big, white *Island Princess.* The mountains turned to rose and then to plum. A cool breeze blew over the decks.

On the sandy beach, the real estate man waved good-by.

Many Happy Returns

Huatabampo—This is one of the great fishing ports on the gulf they call the Sea of Cortez.

The Spanish sailed up here for pearls. They thought the Lower California peninsula was an island.

Eggs rancheros this warm, tropic morning beside the blue, blue sea.

Eggs rancheros are fried. Put on top of a hot tortilla. And splashed with any flavoring the cook has in the kitchen. Tomatoes, onions, hot sauce.

It's a waker-upper all right.

"Ay, Chihuahua! What is in it, waiter? Dynamite?"

Mexican waiters are pleased when tourists bite into the piquant food of Mexico.

Not all Mexican food is blazing with hot sauce. But much of it is—particularly in the North.

The farther north, the spicier. If you want Mexican enchiladas that would blow a safe, go to one of those wonderful places on the river in San Antonio, Texas.

If they'd had those at the Alamo, the battle might have gone the other way.

It is my birthday. "Congratulations, Señor." Happy birthday to me. In this warm land (on birthdays and with fiery eggs rancheros), I take a bottle of Mexico's Bohemia beer.

"It preserves one's youth," said the waiter. "Have another."

"Have one with me," I said.

"Thank you, caballero," he said. (That's me. All caballero. When I shaved this morning, I thought, "Birthdays aren't what they used to be.")

A beer in the a.m. is a festive affair. The warm Mexican

breeze pours through the patio. Happy birthday. I feel better now.

The Jesuit missionaries were first into the long Sonora desert. You find their stone and adobe churches—thick-walled like fortresses—in the little towns off the highways.

The rocky, dirt-tracked road from Mexico City to California followed the trickles of water. The Yaqui and Sonora rivers. They called it *El Camino Real*. The Royal Highway.

It wound up to southern Arizona. Across the Mojave Desert to the Franciscan mission at Our Lady of the Angels of the Earthquakes. (Now we just call it Los Angeles—or L.A. Shame to lose such a fine name.)

From there, El Camino went north as far as Sonoma. South to San Diego—where the first padre died under Indian clubs crying, "Love God, my children!"

"Congratulations on your birthday," said the waiter pouring himself another beer.

He was polite. Birthdays are not celebration days in Mexico.

You celebrate your saint's day. You are named for a saint. And that is the day of the year you celebrate.

I was not named for a saint. I was named for my grandfather who was named for Lincoln's Secretary of War. (Too hard to explain to the waiter in Spanish.)

He was a polite cat. As long as I wanted to celebrate, any day would do for him. As long as the beer held out.

"Already you are looking younger," he said. "Let's have another beer," I said. *"Up with the revolution!"*

"Land and liberty!" said the waiter.

A Night on the Town

Mazatlán—A warm, tropic night in Mazatlán on the West Coast of Mexico. The sunsets are a skyful of vermilion watercolor. Splashing sunsets that dye the entire heavens.

In the last descending sun, people's faces are flushed. The drinks on the table turn pink. The white sand beach has a reddish hue. The world is bathed blood-red.

It is too fierce to bear. Somewhere, the Aztec gods are perishing again; the Spanish captains are on the pyramid temple; the god *Huitzilopochtli* is overthrown; the world is ending.

The sun drops into the sea. There is a sigh all around the room.

Everybody orders. The ice clinks in the glasses, and the waiters come to bustling life.

The swinging place in Mazatlán for years has been The Shrimp Bucket. It is a modest restaurant with windows open to the sea on the waterfront street called Olas Altas—high waves.

The street is a curve, mounting the steep hill where, for many years, the party in power shot the party out of power. (You can't beat that for practical politics.)

We had lunch there. It was so good, we came back in the evening to give the Mexican beer and the Mazatlán turtle eggs a vote of confidence.

The great sea turtles, five-by-five, are laying eggs now in the warm sand.

It is against the law to dig up their eggs. But Mazatlán people have been eating turtle eggs for many years. They are sold door-to-door.

The sea turtle egg is the size and shape of a ping-pong ball. The shell feels like a ping-pong ball, but it dents easily. It dents but is tough. You have to knife it open.

Opened, it looks the same as a chicken egg. Just a little smaller.

The turtle egg gourmet eats them raw.

"I suppose you *could* cook them," said the man in The Shrimp Bucket. "But nobody does."

The way to eat them is open the egg into a small glass. Squeeze Mexican lemon juice on it. (The Mexican lemons look like limes and are the best in the world. I would sell a piece of action on my soul to get such lemons at home.)

Now—You give it a couple dashes of red hot Tabasco sauce.

Drop a couple of pinches of salt on it.

Down the hatch! Fire and fall back.

I don't know why this is such a delicacy. You bang it off too fast to taste the egg—couldn't taste it anyway through that fiery hot sauce and lemon.

The Mazatlán people think it is the greatest thing in the world. Like oysters, they are supposed to be catnip for gentlemen.

The way I take turtle eggs is like everybody else.

Only I have a couple of tequilas beforehand.

You take a small glass of this clear, cactus liquor in your right hand.

In your left hand you take a slice of that wonderful lemon.

Lick the back of your hand in the fold between thumb and finger. Fill this with salt.

Now—lick the salt. Drink the tequila in a gulp. Suck the lemon.

After several tequilas, I took on the turtle egg. (I am chicken about raw chicken eggs. I need plenty of courage for raw turtle eggs.)

After that we had dinner and some more tequila.

A great *mariachi* band came in and played. And I got into a noisy argument with the leader about an Agustin Lara number. I said when he was in love with Maria Feliz he wrote "Madrid" for her. The orchestra leader said he wrote "Maria Bonita."

(I will take that guy up on top of the hill and shoot *him*. He's completely *loco*. It was "Madrid.")

And that's what a sunset and tequila and turtle eggs will do for you on a warm, tropic night at The Shrimp Bucket in the wonderful town of Mazatlán.

Tequila at Sunrise

Mazatlán—On the hill along the Mazatlán waterfront, on the street called Olas Altas, there was a ruined wall from some ancient house.

It was spotted with bullet marks. They were roughly in the shape of a man's body. From the waist to head.

A man who took me there said: "It was where they shot prisoners—only some of the firing squad were poor shots. They just got close."

I said: "Who did they shoot?"

"When the French were here they shot the Mexicans of the Reform," he said. "When the Mexicans won, they shot the French. The Federals shot the revolutionaries during the time of Villa.

"Villa, de la Huerta, Carranza, all of them. They shot the other side."

He said: "Sometimes they shot a criminal. Not often. What crime is so terrible you should be shot?"

I can't find the wall anymore. It's a marvelous view from the hill. The long swells of the Mexican water before it enters the Sea of Cortez.

The rich have built elegant villas on the hill. The wall —where they shot prisoners—must be rubble under them.

The man said: "Before he was shot, the prisoner was given a cigarette. A drink of tequila. It gave him courage. He drank it. He cried: '*Viva Mexico!*' And died."

I went into my beloved pub on Olas Altas. The Shrimp Bucket. They know me. They brought me limes and salt. A bottle of tequila without asking.

I banged it in. I said: "*Viva Mexico!*"

They said: "*Salud!* Where've you been so long?"

I said to the waiter: "Where are the street musicians? Where are the *mariachis*?"

He said:"Ah, we're *muy moderna*. We have a dance band."

As it must to all men (we hope), success hit Chuy and Al between the shoulder blades. Knighted them in the chambers of commerce.

Al and Chuy had the Shrimp Bucket. It was a restaurant in the corner of the little Hotel Siesta. (When I was polishing

brass, the pride of America's merchant fleet, there was a raunchy *cantina* on the corner. I loved it.)

The Shrimp Bucket was a wonderful place. *Mariachis* came off the street. They played Agustin Lara songs for me—*"Mujer." "Consentida." "Granada"*—while I wept in my Bohemia beer.

I ate turtle eggs between tears. You can't get turtle eggs now. Turtles are an endangered species—I helped endanger them, I guess.

They are supposed to be catnip. If a prisoner had eaten turtle eggs he would have shot the *firing* squad.

The Mazatlán oysters are delicious. They are small. In the shell. If you put lemon juice and hot sauce on them, they wince. (Like a prisoner at the wall.)

A little straight tequila goes well with oysters. A little straight tequila goes well with *anything*. (Though I wouldn't want it with a morning firing squad.)

The Mexican morning sun fell into the patio.

Al and Chuy have become successful. They *bought* the hotel. There was a sound of hammers. They're remodeling.

The orchestra came in. They played modern music. The tourists got up and danced.

I said to the waiter:"How about the *mariachis*?" He said sympathetically:"Have another tequila, Señor."

Carnival!

Mazatlán—The Carnival—Mardi Gras—began Saturday night. By Sunday morning, few of the hotel help showed up.

Beds didn't get made. Breakfast orders got mixed up—I got my waffle but never could negotiate some orange juice. Room service did not exist. The coffee was not hot. But the guests were.

At the posh Camino Real, a travel agent name of Alberto sat and had coffee with me.

He said: "What Americans don't realize is that in Mexico the Mexicans feel that Carnival is a time of fiesta. For them." He said: "This is only the beginning. More and more of the hotel people will say to themselves: 'It is Carnival. Why should I work?' "

This is the biggest Carnival in all Mexico. Here and in Vera Cruz. People 'come from all over the Republic. And Mazatlán turns it on for them.

The streets are full of music. *Mariachis*. The strolling street singers. They can be hired to follow you. The agent said: "It is a great thing for a country man to go home and say, 'I led a band for two blocks during Carnival at Mazatlán!' "

"There are *no* fixed rules," some Mexican said about Mexico. It is the Mexican way of life not to be bound to time and schedule.

There is no fixed rule.

At seven in the warm evening, I caught a taxi for Olas Altas, the avenue that fronts the curve of harbor.

"But you must walk about three blocks," said the driver. "It is impossible to enter. *Mucho tráfico*."

The avenue was packed. Bright stands had been set up selling soft drinks. Raw oysters opened on the spot. Spiked with hot sauce. You get a toothpick to winkle them out of the shell.

The stands sell eggs filled with colored confetti. You buy them by the bagful. It is a big thing for girls to sneak up behind you, crush them on your head and disappear into the crowd.

Remember Richard Henry Dana's *"Two Years Before the Mast?"* Same thing with eggshells at the wedding he saw in Santa Barbara in 1834.

And so to The Shrimp Bucket on the corner. Where I had a platterful of frogs legs fresh from the back country. Backed up with tequila and lime and salt.

Mariachi music filling the room and the night on all of Olas Altas.

In the hotel next morning, guests pounded on the tables angrily. Demanded coffee that did not come. Or came hardly warm enough to swim in.

The manager came by. I met him first at the opening of a new hotel at Lake Chapala. That was the night both newly-trained cashiers quit. So did half the new waiters. All from villages around the lake.

They said: "We did not know it would be so much work."

The manager said: "Yes, we are quite short of help." He looked a little pained. (But after the experience at Lake Chapala, what else can happen to you?)

He said to a waiter: "It is better if you *lay* out the knife and fork on the table. Instead of throwing them down in front of the customer."

A guest came up and said: "I do not like my room. I want it changed." (Mazatlán is so full the tourist people are sending them to private homes.)

The agent said: "Remember, too, everybody is a little *cruda*. Hungover. The customers *and* the help."

So we all sat around eating *ceviche*. The soaked-in-lime fish which, with hot sauce, cures you of *la cruda*. You should drink a lot of cold Mexican beer, too. That helps.

The Iguana's Night Off

Puerto Vallarta—In the early morning, the faint beat of engines, the ship's pulse, slowed. And when I pulled the curtains, there was Mexico. Greenly tropical. Coconut palms along the shore. The mountains rising steeply behind the town of Puerto Vallarta.

In the lounge of the cruise ship, a Mexican immigration officer stamped my tourist card. Saw the "journalist" marked on it.

"Ah, he said. *"Leez and Deeck."*

It's been some years since Richard Burton was here with Elizabeth Taylor. But nobody has forgotten.

"You should have seen Puerto Vallarta in the *old* days," says a returning American mournfully. (If one more person says that to me here, I'm going to shoot him.)

I never got to Puerto Vallarta in those good old days. I knew people who came. Mostly adventurous types. You came in on the occasional DC-3 from Guadalajara—there was no road.

Now there's a highway. The airport is one of Mexico's most modern, massive marble and plate glass.

Mexicana, Airwest, Aeromexico all fly in. Several schedules a day. Air France flies in from Paris.

We ferried into shore and caught a taxi out to Puerto Vallarta's El Camino Real. It's one of the new ones of the chain. A sign in the bathroom—in English—tells you the water is purified.

Downtown Puerto Vallarta is stiff with souvenir shops. "English spoken." Restaurants with American music and prices to match.

If there's any of the inexpensive living they used to rave about, I didn't find it.

"It costs much to live here now, Señor," said the taxi driver. (But maybe he was pushing for the tip.)

They made *"The Night of the Iguana"* here. It wasn't the picture but the cast of characters that turned sleepy Puerto Vallarta into a boom town.

Richard Burton, the rough spoken, sexy Welshman.

His new wife, Elizabeth Taylor. Internationally famous for destroying homes and husbands including a few of her own.

Ava Gardner, sultry, with a few blown-up homes and husbands on her form sheet.

The possibility—we hoped probability—that these sex symbols would be at each other's throats (or whatever) fired up newspapers all over the world.

The best reporters flew in. Settled down on the expense account and waited for all hell to break loose in tropical paradise.

The hell of it was that nothing much happened.

The girls didn't fight, tooth and claw for Burton's manly frame. "You couldn't even *talk* to them," a reporter told me. "They were guarded by press agents out of a litter of Doberman Pinschers."

In this frustrating position, everybody sat in Puerto Vallarta's bars and wrote speculation stories.

They rented houses. Prices began to go up.

One reporter speculated that Liz Taylor's makeup covered a black eye. But it was one of those things you write one day, hoping for a denial the next.

Nobody bothered to deny it. Not even the press agents.

So they made *"The Night of the Iguana."* And everybody left. I heard Liz and Dick bought a home here but never came back.

After sunset, we took a drink out on the balcony and watched the big white ship sail into a red sunset. I rather wished I was back on.

Can You Drink the Water Here?

Puerto Vallarta—For a golden day the sun shone on Puerto Vallarta. It's warm as mother love now on the green, tropical coast of Mexico. The sea blue as ink.

The hotel garden is blazing with purple bougainvillea. Red, white and green flowers they call *Bandera de Mexico*—the Mexican flag—because of its colors.

Coconut palms and lacy ferns. Green mountains climb behind the town into a blue sky.

There was a black stormcloud over the Pacific last night. And when I woke in the morning, tropic rain was lashing the sea and shoreline.

In the bricked, open-air dining room, rain dribbled through the thatch. Waiters rushed around mopping the wettest tables. Everybody tried to find a dry seat where the thatch was holding.

The air was warm. No wind. The rain came straight down in drum beats.

Everybody canceled their tours. The big thing in Puerto Vallarta is to go out and see the set where they made *"The Night of the Iguana."*

The coming of Richard Burton and Elizabeth Taylor

changed Puerto Vallarta from a beachcomber's Paradise into one of the most expensive towns in Mexico.

I came down by ship with Al Williams, the San Francisco restaurateur.

After a day's shopping, he told me: "The things they sell here are higher than Mexico City. I think they're higher than Acapulco."

Even with Acapulco prices the tourists rush in.

The *gringos* who were here before moan: "You should have been here before Liz and Dick."

Some of these people from those good old days have opened restaurants.

For them, these are the good old days. They serve local fish—*huachinango*, red snapper—at Stateside prices and thank God that Liz and Dick *did* come here.

At the next table, the thatch overhead gave way and dumped a gallon of water on the lady.

She went out wet and raging. Her husband followed, giving everybody little apologetic smiles. Little pools of water gathered in the low places on the brick flooring.

We found a seat by the sea and ordered rum. It was a good day for pirates.

The lady at the next table said: "I was going to take the tour today. The one to see where they made that picture with Liz and Dick." (Elizabeth Taylor was *not* in the picture. She just came along for the ride. But somehow everybody thinks she was in it.)

She said: "It's too wet out, I guess. I wonder what she's *really* like, Elizabeth Taylor."

I said: "Wild as a pigeon. I got it straight from one of the reporters who was here. They didn't write *everything* that happened."

She was delighted. She said: "That's just what I thought. Anyway, I can always say I was in the same town. Puerto Vallarta."

You Can Say That Again

Puerto Vallarta—A warm, gray morning on the green Mexican coast. A fringe of rain lies over the bay—this should be the last, the rainy season overdue to be over.

The air is damp. Paper slides into the typewriter lightly watersoaked. Even the keys have a wet sound. They don't hit with that dry pop.

The onshore surf at Puerto Vallarta crashes on the warm beach. It costs Acapulco prices to lie on the beach. No refunds when it rains.

In every bar you hear the "if only I had bought that land ten years ago" game.

"Right where the Posada Vallarta is now, out by the airport, I could have had it for a peso a meter. Maybe less."

The second-guessers are full of Bohemia beer and gloomy memories.

The rich life: The aquamarine swimming pool at El Camino Real is set in a garden of flaming bougainvilleas. Coconut palms nod drowsily over the drowsy guests. Suntanning in luxurious beach chairs.

At one end of the pool is the bar. Set under a thatched roof. Seats underwater in the pool at the edge.

Swim over to the bar and sit down. The bartender hands you a big *coco loco*. A green coconut with the top chopped off. Into the coconut milk they toss a lot of ice and gin and vodka—and heaven knows what else.

The guest swims away from the bar with a stagger kick.

The sunsets are magnificent. Gold and red flood the sky. The beach takes on a pinkish hue. People's faces look flushed. There's pink in the glass on your table.

The sun plunges into the sea—you can almost hear it hiss.

Dark comes quickly in the tropics. The lights go on. The waiters rush around with fresh rum drinks.

The Man-Who-Was-Here-Before-Liz-And-Dick says: "I could have had the land at *this* hotel for a couple of thousand pesos. Probablly less than that. But *nothing* was out this far. Just the little village of Puerto Vallarta—you should have seen it then."

A high-priced town these days. A shopkeeper in town told me: "We have a new road now to Guadalajara. But if you want to be *sure* of getting anything, you have to have it flown in.

"Even some of the restaurants have food put down here by plane."

Mexican sportswear, the bright shirts and slacks, are higher here than Mexico City.

The winter season is beginning. Hotels filling up. But even after the season the planes have no problem getting passengers.

Summer is hot as a barbecue pit on the coast. Still tourists come in.

"Soon there will be no season," said the shopkeeper. "Tourists will come all year. So we will all make more money. And prices will go up so we will spend more money.

"The government says it is good for the economy. They say they will make it work. Maybe they know how. But I think only God knows. And in Puerto Vallarta we are far from heaven."

People Who Live in Tin Houses

Manzanillo—We took the road out of Manzanillo beside a mirror lagoon. A forest of lush banana plants was steaming in the morning sun. The taxi driver smelled of rum. But I judged he was only moderately smashed.

Likely a hangover too. For he said sullenly: "Now the rich feel the pinch."

This was 1974 and President Luis Echeverría Alvarez had just announced new taxes: A new car in Mexico would cost a third more. If you made $100,000, the government wanted half.

The driver said: "The rich did not mind when Echeverría passed the tax laws. But now he wants to collect the money. They are indignant."

He blew a little rum at me and his tires screeched as we turned into Las Hadas.

All the cruise ships go into Manzanillo. It's not much of a town. A small central plaza with scrubby palm trees. A statue of a revolutionary hero. Indians from up country sit on the curb, waiting for the rickety bus.

There's a row of palm-thatched open huts across the street. You sit and drink dark beer from Orizaba and they open fresh oysters for you.

It's a hot, low town on the deep blue bay. It slides off into lagoons, and green mountains rise behind it.

When the *Island Princess* put down a gangway, 581 passengers got off. A lot of them got taxis for the half-hour ride to Las Hadas on the other side of the bay.

Las Hadas is a plush hotel. Built by Antenor Patiño, the South American tin maximillionaire.

"It cost 30-million American dollars," said the driver. "Now they will tax it." (And he hummed a few bars of the revolutionary song, "*La Cucaracha.*")

You come in sight of Las Hadas—it means "the fairies"—at a bend in the flowery road.

It's a spectacular sight. Gleaming white. An up-and-down jigsaw of minarets and onion towers. Circular staircases climbing to heaven knows where.

It twists and turns. It makes unpredictable stone stabs in the air. It looks like a palace, ordered by Aladdin from the genii of the lamp. Only the genii had a lousy architect.

Inside, Las Hadas has a marbled look. (There's marvelous Mexican tile but the builders brought in marble from Italy.)

There's a half acre of swimming pool done in circles. Poolside bars serving *piña coladas*.

Like all hotels springing up over Mexico, there's a service problem.

A hotel man told me: "There is no pool of waiters. So we must take our people out of the villages. Now the village boy has always scooped up his beans with a tortilla.

"We put him in a beautiful waiter's uniform. But we have a hard time reminding him that people want spoons on the table."

The waiters were willing. We ordered *ceviche*. Chopped fish in lemon juice, hot sauce, tomato and avocado.

The waiters ran in and out of the kitchen. With glasses. With knives and forks. With napkins. Sometimes they just ran. With everything but food.

I said: "Listen, *amigo*. We must eat. I must get back to the boat."

I got the same driver back. He'd had a few more rums and was in a better mood.

He said: "Señor, would you like to meet some beautiful girls?"

I said: "Man, on that ship there are 581 passengers—500 women and only 81 men. I came ashore for a rest."

The driver let me out at the gangway: "*Dios*, how wonderful to be rich."

And so we sailed away into the sunset.

Barefoot on a Beach

Acapulco—A warm sunny morning in Acapulco. A crazy tourist is swinging from an orange-and-white parachute high in the blue Mexican sky. It's a tourist "attraction." I mean you *pay* to do this.

A speedboat tows you on water skis. You pull the rip cord—Geronimo! And up you go into the wild blue yonder. (What you theenk? I theenk he smoke too much the *ganja.*)

The Rich and Beautiful are flaked out on the golden sand.

The Wise and Wily are under shade. Barefoot.

Acapulco is a-changin'. On a corner of the curving Costera we have Colonel Sanders' Kentucky Fried Chicken. Finger-lickin' good comes out odd in Spanish.

"Who buys it?" I asked.

"Mexicans go mad for it," said the man from Acapulco. "Just like you go to those take-out chile parlors in the U.S."

A couple of Denny's chain restaurants have opened— the Denny Corporation also built a 1000-room hotel. Bring down the American tourists. House them and feed them in your own restaurants.

It's a success story.

What has happened to Acapulco?" I asked. The man from Acapulco said: "It's only a fringe along the beach. Walk back in the *Costa Chica* hills and it's like Butch Cassidy and the Sundance Kid.

"Why only a couple of years ago a bunch of bandits rode out—on horses, mind you!—and held up the *Estrella de Oro.* The Mexico City bus."

He said: "There are some of those towns in the back

country that are run by gunmen. I wouldn't drive the main highway at night for anything."

The State of Guerrero has a reputation for violence. This is where Zapata recruited the tough little Indians in white pajama suits. They rode through the country beating the boots off the uniformed Federal troops.

On back roads you drive by falling-down *hacienda* walls, still marked by smoke and flame.

He said: "Tourist Acapulco is a thin line along the beach. Behind that is Mexico."

In the morning we buy lottery tickets. The national lottery is every Mexican's dream. Haven't you heard of the poor Indian whose first prize brought him a million pesos? (You will.)

The prizes are printed in the newspapers. Fortune brushed close a couple of times. But not enough to take the lint off my suit.

"Here is a pretty number, Señor," says the lottery ticket seller.

For a dollar you can have 24 hours dreaming of coming fortune. Where else in the world can you buy happiness at such a price?

The waiter came by. He said: "Did you hear about the poor Indian who bought the winning lottery ticket?"

I said: "And won a million pesos?"

I added: "A poor Indian wins every day—how else could they sell lottery tickets without that story?"

The man from Acapulco said: "I wish I were a poor Indian. I've been playing the lottery for eighteen years. I haven't won yet."

Flat Side of the Tortilla

Acapulco—A blue sky morning at Acapulco. The milk-run jet to Mexico City, on climbing power, swings over the long sand beach.

Breakfast comes up to the balcony: *Huevos rancheros*— eggs ranch style. Sunny-side up on a tortilla. Sprinkled with hot sauce and lime juice. It's an eye opener.

In the breezy bar, last night's Life of the Party is opening his eyes with a *coco loco*. A big splash of Mexican rum in a fresh coconut half. *Buenos dias, Señor!*

My hotel is a replica of a Mayan temple. (Looks like the big one at Tikal.) If the ancient Mayans could see us now, they'd turn in their basketball suits.

The Mayans played basketball. Winners got to *kill* the losers. You can't beat that for sportsmanship.

Behind us are the green Guerrero hills. Not as peaceful as they look.

"There's always some shooting in Guerrero," says the American who lives here. "The people from Guerrero are much like the old Wild West cowboys of America.

"There are towns back there that are practically ruled by gunmen—you have to be handy with a pistol just to *run* for mayor.

"A Supreme Court judge was shot in a hotel a little while ago. A Mexico City bus was held up by men on *horseback*! Just rode out of the hills and held it up."

At Chilpancingo on the road to Mexico City, the rector of the State University has been kidnaped.

None of this affects the jet set fringe of beach. And few people get off the beach farther than the Costera. The long beach road follows the curve of the blue bay. Flowery. Divided by a strip of trees. Lined with high-rise hotels. Elegant shops. Expensive restaurants.

A few years ago, I drove out on a gravel road on the side of the green mountains. So high that we were in clouds and pine trees. The road dropped off sharply. You could look down and see sugar cane at the bottom.

The town is Ixcateopan. And in the old, old church from Spanish days, they had the bones of Cuauhtemoc. The last Aztec emperor.

Or so they say. Cortez captured him and tortured him, looking for lost Aztec gold.

At last on a hot and angry day, he hanged him.

The legend is that Indians brought the body back to Ixcateopan. His birthplace.

These are Indian towns. The people speak an Indian dialect. (The Government puts in schools. The children learn Spanish.)

They are short and squat, wearing rough, white cotton pajama-like coats and pants. Leather sandals. The tire-tread soles print "Goodyear" in the dust.

These are the people Zapata raised for the revolution.

Tough, enduring guerilla cavalrymen. On ruined, deserted *hacienda* walls, you can see the fire scars they left behind.

The American said: "The first thing you do if you go into politics in Guerrero is hire yourself a bodyguard. A *pistolero* they call them here."

None of this ferment reaches the beaches.

The weather is splendid now. And the modern jets come to the modern airport, high above the sugar cane villages and the charcoal burners and the Indian towns and the gray bones of Cuauhtemoc.

Happiness is a Cold Coco Loco

Acapulco—Warm winter now in Acapulco. And at the open-air bar in the posh Princess Hotel a tourist lady says: "Can you drink the water here?"

A man at the next table said: "It's okay here. They've got a filter system or something. I wouldn't drink it in town."

He ordered himself a Coco Loco. They chop the top off a green coconut. Pour a yard of rum in it.

He said: "The way I figure it, the rum kills the bugs."

She said: "What do you think about brushing your teeth?"

"Use Coca-Cola," he said.

He took a long sip from the coconut. He said to me: "I used to sit around and worry. What about the ice? How do you know the bottled water is filtered? Maybe the maid didn't want to go downstairs. She filled it from a tap."

He said: "How can you get anything from these Coco Locos? Rum and coconut milk—it's organic probably. *Everything's* organic nowadays. Full of vitamins.

He looked like he had a hangover. He was probably at *my* party last night.

We've been sailing down here in the pathway of Francis Drake. Mainly floating on a sea of margaritas. Salt-rimmed glass filled with iced tequila, Cointreau and lemon.

We came down on a cruise ship with Robert Power, a Drake's history buff and president of the California Historical Society.

Just before sailing, the tequila people sent out ten cases of that extraordinary liquor that fueled a dozen revolutions.

Al Williams, the Mexican restaurateur, went into Los Angeles and bought a couple of thousand Mexican snacks. Little tortillas wrapped around spicy meat.

Last night we had a party. I think the man at the next table was there. Neither of us can remember.

Fame and fortune. Drake took a shipload of a silver from the *"Cacafuego"*. He took a load of treasure from a town 200 miles south of here—Gualtulco.

He even took the church bells—Francis didn't overlook anything.

The man at the next table said to the waiter: "I'll have another Coco Loco. Something happened to my head last night. I went to a ship's party, and whoever gave it spiked my drinks."

I said: "They ought to put people like that in jail."

He said: "Some nut who's following Francis Drake around. Why would anybody do that?"

I said: "It takes all kinds."

It's warm but rainy in Acapulco. Manhattan West. In this Mexican town—there was a *cantina* on the corner.

They had never heard of margaritas. The rum came pure and white. You didn't have to worry about the ice. There wasn't any.

There are no Fixed Rules

Acapulco—He stood on the jetty at Acapulco waiting for the launch load of passengers from the cruise ship *Island Princess*. He wore tailored blue slacks and a rose-colored shirt. He looked well-fed and prosperous.

He said:"Taxi, Señor?"

He took my bags to the street—the Costera Boulevard that circles the blue, blue bay. But he didn't put my bags in his car. He flagged a passing taxi. "He's a friend of mine."

The taxi driver drove me out to the Hotel Paraiso Marriott. "That's $4." Later I caught a taxi off the street and went back to the jetty to meet friends. The correct price is 80 cents.

In that wonderful book, "*Viva Mexico,*" the author asks an Indian workman about local customs and prices.

The workman thought about it and he said: "*No hay reglas fijas.*" "There are no fixed rules." When you absorb this, you know Mexico.

Along the great curve of the Costera, high-rise hotels shut off the bay. There is one open spot—a half block long.

A man I know said: "Everybody is trying to get that and build a hotel. But it is a graveyard. The gravestones are gone. It is only empty land. But people say: 'My great-great-grandfather is buried there. Would you build a hotel on his bones?' "

In Acapulco the menus carry the prices in pesos and

U.S. dollars. The taxi driver quotes you the fare in dollars.

Room information is written in both languages.

The Indian woman—short, squat, wearing the village blouse—holds up a lacy dress and says: "It is only $30."

"Taxes are killing us," said the man from Acapulco. "Income tax is up. And they want us to pay it. Well, naturally, we always had income tax. But we only declared what we wanted to. Now they look at the books."

He said: "Gasoline was 64 cents. They tax it and make it 96 cents a gallon. They tax homes and water.

"*No hay reglas fijas.*" I was ripped off four times in one day. As smoothly as the magician pulls the rabbit from the hat.

It was embarrassing. I thought I knew this town—I've been here often enough.

Had my bill raised by a waiter. Was pushed around by the men who run those parachutes towed by a boat.

"I know I said $10, Señor. But that is for the parachute ride. It is $10 more for the boat. And the boy on the beach should get a tip."

"There are no fixed rules."

Cabañas, the bandit, is still at large in the green hills behind Acapulco. (He would do better in town. Buy a pair of blue slacks, a rose shirt and hail taxis.)

Still it's a beautiful bay. (Though you must get in a high room in the hotel to see it.)

The sun goes down rapidly in a shower of red and gold. The islands are black against the evening sky.

The Costera is a long necklace of lighted jewels.

It costs—this pearl of the Pacific. But pearls don't come cheap. Look at the overhead for the oysters.

The North

In Mexico the village people consult brujas, hechizeras and curanderas. Brujas are witches. They can put a curse on your enemy. (But another bruja can neutralize it.) Hechizeras—something like wizards. They can give you love potions. (Put a few drops in her Coca Cola and watch the Señorita melt twice as fast as ordinary aspirina.)

Curanderas are the wrinkled Indian women who sit in the markets with a pile of curing herbs in front of them. They can cure you of flat feet and grow hair on a turnip.

There's an amazing virility builder of dried snake tea. If you've got the virility to drink it down.

Rootin' Tootin' Sonofagun

Parrál—When I arrived in Parrál it was the anniversary of the death of Pancho Villa, almost half a century ago.

There was a ceremony in Mexico City. Some speeches at the monument. It's only been a few years that official Mexico has recognized the Centaur of the North.

A Mexican in Chihuahua told me: "You see Villa was a hero of the Revolution. But to the U.S., he was the man who shot up the Army post at Columbus, New Mexico. To many Americans—many Mexicans, too—he was a large size bandit."

He said: "So for those who are for glorifying him, we keep a statue of him in Chihuahua. For those against, we call it by the name of the Army—the *Gran División del Norte*."

The thing was resolved a few years ago by the Mexican Congress. They declared that General Francisco Villa was a Grade-A hero of the Revolution.

The Mormon Church beat them to it. Shortly after Villa was shot from behind the hay bales in Hidalgo del Parrál, he posthumously became a member of the Latter Day Saints.

(This is pretty exclusive and will probably shake up the historians.)

There was an elderly man in California, a former Mormon missionary in Mexico, and he said: "I was in Mexico during the Revolution. Several times I had occasion to talk to the General. I made it a point to drop in some explanation of the Book of Mormon—though that was not the original purpose of our conversation."

The Church of Latter Day Saints enters people after death. Mormons trace their ancestry. The located ancestor becomes a member of the church with a passport to everlasting glory.

The old missionary said: "I felt that the General was interested. But in war there's not much time for missionary work. I had time; he didn't."

He said after Villa was assassinated—gunned out of his car, sightless eyes staring into the blue Chihuahua sky—he went to visit the widow.

(He didn't say which widow. Villa was a rootin' tootin' sonofagun. He married on whim. There are still several widows living.)

He said: "I mentioned talking to the General about our

church." (The Mormons say the Indians here are descendants of the Lost Tribes of Israel.) She said to me: "Just a few days before he was killed, the General spoke of his disappointment that he could not have learned more. That it was the religion he could feel in his heart."

The missionary said: "On the strength of this, I made a report. Francisco Villa was made a member of the Church forever."

We flew into Parrál. They were having the first parade for Pancho Villa. Not official Mexico. Just some of the veterans of the *Gran División del Norte*.

It's a hot, dusty desert town—an unimportant place to die.

The veterans marched slowly. It was a long time ago when they rode with Villa—1914-1916.

They marched out to the cemetery where the General is buried. The flatstone on the grave says:

"There are some who would detract from his fame and honor; but by doing so they only show how small they are."

It is signed by the chief of his *Dorados*—The Golden Ones, the bodyguard:

It says: "*Presente, mi General!*"

It was after this I picked up the story of the Mormon missionary. A lot of Mormons left Salt Lake for Mexico when the church outlawed polygamy.

The Mormons who stuck with polygamy got the right man in Villa—he married the girls. A friend said to him once: "You know there are plenty of girls. You don't have to *marry*."

Pancho Villa said: "I do not drink from public fountains."

Yaqui Country

Ciudad Obregón—Ciudad Obregón is a cotton town on the West Coast of Mexico. They are reclaiming the Sonora desert, mile after mile, with dammed water.

There are still hundreds of miles of primitive land. Tarahumara Indians who cut their hair shoulder-length and wear a home-woven cotton kilt.

The fierce Yaquis are gone. Or are left only in mixed bloodlines and in names: the Rio Yaqui. They had a game so funny it would kill you—which it did.

They took captured Federal soldiers and sliced the soles off their feet. Then they stuck them with cactus thorns until they got up and tried to run.

They were tough, indestructible desert Indians. They never surrendered.

This town was named for General Obregón. One of the General-Presidents who came out of the Revolution.

"Revolutions begin in the north," is a Mexican saying.

The northerners are desert-bred. They are horse soldiers—paved highways and cars are a recent thing in this part of Mexico.

They wear the big curving brim hats you see in the movies. Big enough to hold a gallon of water.

They rode through the desert, up the plateau and to the capital to the tune of "*La Cucaracha*"—the cockroach.

> *"He cannot march anymore.*
> *He can't, because he hasn't got*
> *Marijuana to smoke."*

The desert marches down to the coast. Then the land turns marshy and fills with mangrove trees. Thick growth, half in and half out of the water.

Mosquitoes. Little biting gnats called *jejenes*. They leave an itching welt that lasts for a week. And then there was malaria.

Now they've sprayed for mosquitoes. The coast lands are white with cotton. The Mexican peso is hard currency.

The Generals seem to be out of politics. In recent elections, Mexico has elected lawyers.

I hate to see the desert go. But this is still wonderful Mexico. Where gas stations run out of gas. The restroom is out of order. The swimming pool is advertised grandly. But the water doesn't run.

You get a boy to watch your car. And you come back and find he's washed it. "Watch" and "wash" sound much alike in a Mexican accent. When you say "watch," put a forefinger on your lower eyelid and pull it down.

Mexicans talk a lot with their hands.

Pull an imaginary beard. Means, "There's a pretty girl!" The Mexican waitress puts her thumb and forefinger a quarter inch apart: "Wait just a minute."

Bang your elbow on your fist: "Stingy fellow. Didn't leave a tip."

If another driver cuts in front of you, show him your fist with a thumb and little finger extended. Like horns. *That* is very nasty.

The Army is no longer on horseback. They use jeeps. Officers don't carry the elegant handmade swords from Oaxaca.

The revolutionary swords are hung on library walls. A reminder of wilder days. They are polished like silver and bear a carved inscription:

> "When this viper bites in the moment of heat,
> There is no remedy in the drugstore or
> Prescription of the doctor."

Rings Faint the Spanish Gun

Arizpe—Stick a shovel into Mexico almost anywhere and you lift it dripping with historic treasure.

Take the Lost Sobara mine, for instance—.

"You see," said the storekeeper of this little North Mexico town, "the Spanish did not wish the Mexicans to enjoy their treasure. So when we won our freedom they hid the mines—ah, the rich mines! Gold! Silver!"

"And could one encounter them again, Señor?" I asked.

"Naturally," he said. "Lost mines are always encountered again. Usually by visions. Sometimes by dreams. Ah, the riches of the Lost Sobara! A vein of silver three feet thick!

"And it is clearly written in the records: *'From the mine entrance, the miners could see the principal entrance of the Arizpe cathedral.'* "

We flew to Arizpe for the great discovery of the tomb of Captain Juan Bautista de Anza. Spanish soldier. Military Governor of the West. Founder—with 240 ragged colonists and wild longhorn cattle—of San Francisco.

He was buried in the cathedral when this cattle town of 1500 (today) was the bustling frontier capital of everything from Mexico City to Oregon.

"You came to see the bones of the Captain?" asked the storekeeper.

He serves the community in a small, baked adobe building—two rooms. One for chaps and leather quirts and coiled rope. Iron hinges, staples for barbed wire, crowbars.

The other room is for gallantry: Shaving lotion so powerful you can smell it across the Rio Sonora; cowboy hats (they favor the center crease of Arizona here rather than the enormous brim of Pancho Villa and the Chihuahua country); dress shirts and a rack of ties.

Mexican cowboys in heavy leather chaps tie their horses outside while they shop for something to catch the Señoritas' eyes.

"You come to see the famous grave?"

"Tell me about the gold," I said. I go wild for lost mines.

"It is weather like this," said the storekeeper confidently, "that uncovers the treasures of Spain."

The Sonora winds have been blowing the unpaved streets into dusty tunnels between the flat-roofed, one-story houses.

"The winds blow off the covering put there by the Spaniards. Oh, if I had time I would go and look, myself. But I must tend the store."

It is knowledge like this that will make me a rich man some day. The treasures I know about are unbelievable. (However, I believe it.)

In Morelia, Mexico, there is a tunnel leading to the cathedral. It is stuffed with hidden gold bars. I know a man who saw it. His father was digging a well and broke right into it.

The gold was so bright it dazzled him.

"But my father said it was cursed. So he covered it up again."

There is a shipload of pearls on the coast of Lower California. You ask me why we haven't found it.

Well, it is inland, that is why. The coastline has changed. The shipwreck is several miles inland. Under sand dunes. If I didn't have to tend the store—

The Spanish were great conquistadors but mighty poor colonizers. That is why they lost (and buried) the riches of the Americas. They left a legacy of high interest rates.

"Indeed," said the storekeeper, "we pay 12 per cent for a short loan. And if one falls behind, it becomes from 18 to 24 per cent. Clearly if one cannot find a lost mine one should open a bank, no?"

Down the Hatch

Culiacán—All along the West Coast of Mexico I've been trying to buy *bacanora*. "Ah, Señor," they say, "you must go to the town of Bacanora."

This is not absolutely true. They distill mountain moonshine all over the northern State of Sonora. They *say* the best comes from Bacanora. But people in the inland towns, where Father Kino's stone missions stand on dusty plazas, will argue that *their* town makes the absolutely, guaranteed, pure, delicious *bacanora*.

"*Bacanora* was invented by the Indians," one man told me. "No, it was invented by the missionaries, the Jesuit padres," said his friend.

You cannot buy it commercially. It is unlicensed. Illegal. Pays no taxes. It is full of the same fierce Independence that sent our colonists into the Whiskey Rebellion.

It is made from *agave*, the spiky, gray century plant cactus. Same as *pulque* or *tequila* or *mescal*.

The makers claim it has better taste. And unusual qualities.

"Men of eighty drink *bacanora* and become new fathers."

After three *bacanoras*. The man who told me this offered to drive me to a village—"not far from here, Señor"—where a man 100 years old had just fathered a tot.

"It also cures rheumatism," he said. "It cures many things. Almost *any*thing."

He said it was a powerful liniment. You could rub it on a sprain and walk away laughing.

All of Mexico's cactus drinks have special qualities. The Spaniards found the Indians drinking *pulque*. It's a mild fermentation, about the strength of beer.

The Aztecs worshiped a tequila goddess. There's a temple on a hill not far from Mexico City.

Tequila comes from the Guadalajara region in Jalisco State. You can get aged tequila—*tequila añejo*. But Mexicans say you only get it in Jalisco. The stuff shipped out is aged chemically.

In Culiacán, tequila is the drink.

You drink it straight with lemon and salt to lick on the side. Or with a hot sauce chaser called *sangrita de la viuda*—the blood of the widow.

Some people put a drop or two of seasoning sauce in it. Maggi is the favorite in Mexico.

Tourists drink it as margaritas: tequila, lemon, triple-sec and ice. Rim a wet cocktail glass with salt and pour the drink in it.

Down south in Oaxaca they make *mescál*. It is bottled in black ceramic pots, and they drop a cactus worm in each bottle. They say it improves the taste. (The joke is whoever gets the worm pays for the drinks.)

Bacanora distillers say *their* liquor doesn't need aging—it is that fine.

"Just distill it and let it get cool enough to drink."

In this ancient town, the explorer Coronado outfitted his men before he set off for two years of wandering in the American southwest. Looking for the Seven Cities of Cibola.

Each man was to carry certain equipment. It is listed in the archives: So many stirrups and bits; so much meal; so many pieces of armament. They were also to carry a certain amount of "the wine of the country."

The mescál people say it was mescál. The tequila people say:"*Que va!* It was tequila!" The bacanora people say, "When he got to northern Sonora he threw everything away and used *bacanora. That* is why he kept going for two years."

Mexico City

I brought a case of Irish whiskey to Mexico on St. Patrick's Day. And in Bill O'Dwyer's penthouse—(he'd been Mayor of New York and Ambassador to Mexico)—everybody had a sentimental drink to the San Patricio Battalion.

They were Irish immigrants, enlisted in the United States Army. When they found themselves in the Mexican war in 1848, some deserted and joined the Mexican Army. It was more easy-going and this is a Catholic country.

When Mexico City fell, they were captured. The American Army took them up on the hill of Chapultepec. They put ropes around their necks. The last thing they saw was the morning sun coming up over the snowy volcanos. The American flag rising above the Presidential palace.

Then the hangman lashed the horses and drove the wagon out from under them.

Buenos Dias, Cortez

Mexico, D.F.—It was just about dusk when the jet plane slid over the sunset-pink Mexican mountains and began the let down into the Valley of Anáhuac.

The approach by air was the same that Cortez made by foot and horse, with sword and cross, in the great conquest 457 years ago.

Down the steep, sloping gap between the volcanoes; over the gleaming canals of Chalco and Xochimilco—the last of the great waterways that fed the Aztec capital.

A round swing over the broad boulevards that once were causeways; over Texcoco—here Cortez launched his boats to hold the great lake of Mexico.

And so, with a gentle bump, onto Mexico City's modern steel-and-glass airport.

In the past twenty five years, Mexico City has changed violently from the Spanish colonial to the modern. It spouted a cloud of antique dust as old stone buildings fell. It clattered with riveting guns as steel beams fell into new skyscrapers.

We taxied in through the old town in the deepening evening.

Through the narrow streets in the shadows of the buildings left by Royal Spain. (The modern, tourist section lies further out.)

This is slum area now. A colorful slum area—I suppose it is not so colorful if you have to live there.

Streets full of Mexican language. Bumper-to-bumper buses. (With bumper-to-bumper passengers.) Full of lantern-lit stands selling hot tortillas wrapped around hotter green chiles.

Full of cries of lottery ticket sellers: "Today! Today! Three million pesos!"

The driver shaved two crosswalking Indians close enough to put a foot in heaven. He jammed the brakes at the de Cortés Hotel and announced the fare was now seven pesos.

"Señor," I said, "the fare has always been ten pesos for a private taxi, all to myself. Here I share the ride with five others."

"Times have changed," said the driver proudly. "This is the new fare in the new Mexico."

"It is also the custom to tip the chauffeur," he added pointedly.

"Heaven help Mexico," I said. I gave him another peso.

So modern times come to the capital that was the Aztec Tenochtitlán: New fares. Tipping for taxi drivers. (Twenty years ago, before taximeters, we bargained each ride before mounting.)

"We even have smog," said my bellboy. "Just like Los Angeles."

I stay at the Hotel de Cortés as the last outpost against the approach of the modern city.

It stands on an ancient street, surrounded these days by huge medical signs promising quick cure for V.D.

But in the flagstone patio, on the pillared balconies, the moonlight falls softly.

And over the old stone walls into this sanctuary comes the sound of the temple bells that Cortez cast with silver alloy to give them a sweeter sound.

Café con Leche

Mexico, D.F.—On the sad night some 450 years ago, a Spanish gentleman by name Pedro Alvarado was hurrying along the street just outside my door.

He was hurrying for the very good reason that a number

of Aztecs were hustling along behind him. With some very sharp spears.

When Alvarado got to that part of my street that is now called "The Leap of Alvarado," there was no bridge. He thereupon put his lance in the bottom of the lake and pole vaulted the chasm. So the story goes.

We are having *café con leche*—coffee with hot milk— this sunny Mexican morning in the courtyard of the Hotel de Cortés.

The Hotel de Cortés was once a monastery—the monks were devoted to the mentally ill of Mexico City. I imagine a good many people who sat here were a little off their rockers. (I feel a little giddy myself. But it may be the altitude.)

In the Spanish style, the rooms are around the central patio. The antique pillars are covered with ivy. And in the center of the patio there is a tinkling fountain.

The Olympic leaps of these modern days are when you cross the street where Cortez and Alvarado retreated on that *Noche Triste*.

It is a broad street now. The taxis panting like so many bulls at the red light. If you can make it across the street before the light turns green, you win. If you don't—leap!

The pedestrian in Mexico City is big game. When you step off the sidewalk, you are in open season.

My street is alongside the shady park called the Alameda —but on the wrong side.

On the other side of the park is the fashionable Avenida Juárez. Chrome-and-glass tourist hotels. Silver shops. Leather goods. Cut stones from the gem cutters of Querétaro.

On my side are the cheap jewelry stores. Street corner stands selling tacos and *pozole*—the Mexican dish of corn and pork that is supposed to cure the hangover.

Stores selling guitars. Secondhand typewriters and brassy home fixtures. Oil cans cut down into charcoal stoves. Cheap tobacco. Gray stone churches built by the conquistadors and still showing cannon fire marks of the Revolution.

Windows full of plaster saints. Photographers with windows full of portrait pictures colored lavishly by hand. Gilt signs of doctors specializing in quickie blood tests.

Along this street, the greedier soldiers with Cortez fell in the canals between the bridges and sank. Weighted down with Aztec gold.

When the workmen dig in this street, the archaeologists come down and sit by the excavations.

Did Pedro really leap the canal? You can get a lot of arguments from the historians.

After the Conquest and after Pedro died—(a horse fell on him while he was chopping up Indians)—the Alvarado relatives went to court about it.

They took testimony. And the court decided Pedro did vault the canal.

Surviving Aztecs testified that they were so astonished as the vaulter sailed over them, they stuffed their mouths with dirt. This being what Aztecs did when astonished.

But said the historian-soldier of that day, Bernal Diaz: "For my part I aver that he could not have leaped it in any manner.

"But, as some will insist on the reality of it, I repeat it again, it could not have been done. And let those who wish to ascertain it view the place; the bridge is there and the depth of water will prove no lance could reach the bottom."

I went out to look at the place. But it is dry as a bone today. A taxi nearly got me en route. But I leaped.

Where the Heart Is

Mexico, D.F.—Just down the street from my Mexico City hotel, workmen are tearing up one of the old buildings.

"Possibly under there is where they will find the lost gold," said the waiter who brings my coffee on the patio. "The lost gold of Montezuma."

That is quite possible. On my street, Cortez retreated on the Sad Night, losing all the loot in the lake alongside the causeway to Tacuba.

"Accordingly, I got together all the gold and jewels belonging to Your Majesty," Cortez wrote to the Spanish King, *"and placed them in a separate room, where I had them made up into various bundles, and handed them over to certain officials of Your Majesty whom I specially appointed in Your Majesty's name."*

By the time he reached the mainland at Tacuba, 150 Spanish soldiers and some 2000 Indian allies had been killed at the bridges.

"All the gold, jewels, clothing and other things we were carrying were lost, and in addition the guns."

After the Conquest, the Spanish searched vainly for the lost treasure.

Neither search nor torture turned up more than a few pieces.

"How do you know the treasure was lost at that bridge?" I asked the waiter.

"It was the first bridge that was cut," he said. "Who sinks in the water fastest? The man who is loaded with gold. While we talk here," said the waiter, "some lucky workman may be sinking his shovel toward the gold.

"I should be down there myself with such a feeling in my heart—a feeling such as I had the day I won 2000 pesos on the lottery. What a day that was!"

Our street is called by various names: Where Cortez entered it, behind the Cathedral, it is called Tacuba. In front of our hotel, it is called Hidalgo. A few blocks further on, it becomes "The Leap of Alvarado."

"Perhaps the gold was lost where Alvarado made his famous leap?" I said.

"I don't think the gold got that far," said the waiter.

"Most of the treasure was loaded on a Spanish mare. A

mare, loaded with gold, must have sunk like a stone to the bottom. Who knows where that happened. Perhaps under where I am now standing."

"I am blessed and cursed with extremes of luck," said the waiter. "Once I dreamed of three auto buses coming directly at me.

"To dream in threes is tremendously lucky. I went out and bought a lottery ticket. The ticket that won was exactly the reverse numbering of mine.

"The dream was correct. But I had forgotten that the buses were coming toward me. If they had passed and been going away, I would have bought the right number."

"Lately, I have been dreaming of beans. This is the way treasure is often disguised in a dream. Beans are the riches of Mexico. Beans and corn.

"Such dreams mean I am very close to wealth."

After breakfast, I went down to look at the excavation. "Any luck?" I asked one of the workmen. "Any Spanish gold?"

"You come from the hotel?" he said. "Ah, you have been listening to the waiter. The one who tells tourists of his luck and gold.

"Oh, to be a waiter!" said the workman. "He makes as much in an hour as I do in a whole day, slaving with the shovel. Just for serving tourists. That and a wornout story of gold."

Chance of a Lifetime

Mexico, D.F.—"It's not the water," said the tourist lady at the next table. "It's the altitude."

The other lady said: "I think it's the ice."

They both shook some pills onto the breakfast table and popped them in. Thus we protect ourselves against the dread *turista*. Happy holidays.

We went down to Prendes in the old part of Mexico City the other night. Down where the streets narrow and antique churches of New Spain ring iron bells—bong! bong! bong!

We don't worry about our health at Prendes. We drink the water. We fortify ourselves with straight tequila. It is better than penicillin. (Tastes better too.)

The restaurant is not big with tourists. Wrong part of town. Brightly lit and tiled. It is jammed at lunch with Mexican businessmen. But at night there are few people.

When the President of Mexico gives a party, Prendes caters it.

No country has had more publicity about health problems than Mexico. Tourists come here with pills enough to open a drugstore.

They have the latest scam from the doctor.

Even American doctors are affected. Doctors have given

me all kinds of advice. Some are nervous as any tourist lady. Some are philosophical: "If you get it, take these."

Mexico made efforts a few years ago to change the image. A Mexican doctor insisted the internal distress was caused by altitude.

"Spend the first few days quietly," he said. "Take afternoon naps."

At Prendes they bring tequila—the clear, white tequila—with lemon and salt. On the side they bring a slice of cheese and some radishes.

"Don't eat anything raw that you don't peel yourself," say the guidebooks. [I write that myself sometimes. But I don't pay attention to what I write.]

I eat the radishes. I've been eating at Prendes many a healthy year. I don't want to break my luck.

True that people have come down with internal distress in Mexico. I don't think it's as widespread as the publicity.

You don't say that to visitors though. Most tourists are convinced the *turista* is issued with the tourist card. Only the pocketful of pills keeps them alive.

"My doctor gives me these," said the tourist lady. "One before each meal." Her pills were green demons.

The other lady shook out *her* pills—red devils. She said her doctor told her to take one *after* meals.

Americans who live here get a touch once in awhile. But one of them told me: "People get the same thing in Pasadena. They come down here and they *expect* to get something.

"It's part of the adventure. They go home and say: 'First we went to the museum. Then we went to dinner. Then I didn't feel very well. Then I took my pills. Then I was all right.' "

There's a bunch of doctors with offices in one of the big tourist hotels. They are all becoming wealthy, passing out pills and sympathy.

High and Dry

Mexico, D.F.—In the sunny Mexican morning, the tourists lay out their day's quota of pills beside the steaming coffee.

Mexico is heaven for pill makers. No tourist comes to

Mexico without a glorious, scary feeling that he is riding a roller coaster of chance on his internals.

Gallons of ink have been shed on the health problem. And no tourist intends to be cheated of his right to go home, boasting of bugs that churned his insides like an ice cream freezer.

He expects the bug to be issued with the tourist card. And he carries a pharmaceutical wardrobe for the good fight.

"The real health problem here," said the Mexican hotel manager, "is not the bug they call 'Montezuma's revenge.'

"It is the common hangover—*la cruda* we call it.

"The tourist arrives. They give him a margarita of tequila at the airport.

"He gets to the hotel and he says: 'I think I will have one beer. Because I hear it is good for you at this altitude.'

"For dinner he has some Mexican rum.

"Next morning he gets up. He is *crudo*. 'I've got it!' he says. 'The Mexican bug. It must be the water.'

"He forgets he has not touched the water yet. Only tequila, beer and rum."

If the hangover is the problem, this is the land of the cures.

"You can take *menudo* at one of the little stands in the old part of town," said the hotel man. "It is an absolute cure. It is soup. Made very strong from the stomachs of beef cattle. It is full of very hot peppers.

"Then we have *pozole*. This is pork meat. Chopped and cooked with a kind of bleached corn—like your hominy.

"This makes a soup. And on top you put red chile powder and chopped onions and some oregano. A half dozen sardines. Slices of avocado. One dish and you are cured."

I have had this sovereign dish myself. It is delicious. I asked the hotel man if he hadn't forgotten an important item.

"Of course," he said striking his head with his hand. "You always take the *pozole* with mescal."

Mescal is something like tequila. It is made from the spiky cactus that keeps Mexico in hangovers.

It comes from Oaxaca. From the south. And it is bottled in black earthenware jars of the region.

In each bottle, the mescal makers drop one cactus worm. They have some excellent reasons for this: Flavor, strength, custom, etc.

And if you draw the worm when they pour the mescal, it is a sure cure. You quit drinking. (At least I did.)

There are also cures that involve herbs boiled with cinnamon sticks. I recall (but never tried) "the bull."

"Eat green chilis and drink the bool," said the waiter

who gave me this recipe. "Do this and you will never suffer from the *crudo*. You will live forever."

Take one bottle of light beer. Put it in a stein. Add one-quarter bottle of ginger ale and one-quarter bottle of orange crush.

"Then," said the waiter—who admitted he was slightly *crudo* at the suffering same moment, "you must put in a couple of drinks of Mexican rum. Mix this and drink it and you will be well."

Said the hotel manager: "These are the things the tourist should take. Not the green pills. The yellow pills. The red pills.

"Strong *menudo*. *Pozole* with rich mescal. The bull you speak of sounds as if it had its wonders.

"Naturally," said the hotel man, "I would not tell a tourist he had a hangover instead of some rare Mexican ailment. It would be bad for the tourist business.

"The tourist wishes to feel that he is at war with illness. And only his bravery and a couple of pills are saving him. We should advertise these imagined ills. He will be *crudo* anyway. And that will prove it to him."

Man with the Pistola

Mexico, D.F.—A grim smoggy morning in Mexico City. Seven million people. Endless lines of cars spitting exhaust. Buses trailing black diesel fumes. Charcoal cooking. They put a smoky lid on the blue sky city the Aztecs called Tenochtitlán.

Man cannot live without throwing beer cans on the land.

Bernal Diaz del Castillo, the soldier-historian, recalled the palaces of the lake city: "*I was a young man then, and I thought I should never see such wonders. But alas, now all is destroyed, and what were once noble gardens are nothing but a field of Indian corn.*"

The old part of Mexico City is run-down, shabby. But there are remains of the stone palaces built by the Spanish conquerors. Intricate carving on pillars of pink *tezontle* stone.

The rain spouts are carved like cannon and bear on the street.

The courtyards are enormous and the wheel ruts are deep in the stone entrances.

These are what remain from the sword-swinging men

from the barren plains of Estremadura who brought the Cross and slavery to Mexico.

In all Mexico today there is no monument to Cortez. And in Guatemala there is no statue of Alvarado.

In both cities, the chief statues are those of the last Indian kings.

"In Latin America they may admire the man on horseback. The man with the gun," said the man from Acapulco. "That is why so many Presidents have been Army Generals.

"That is why Latin America doesn't think much of your wars and riots and civil disorders. They think, 'America has the soldiers, the guns, the bombs. Why don't they go in with everything and restore peace with the *pistola*?"

"The pistol is the dear love of the Latin American. With the pistol he maintains justice. He kills his enemy. He protects himself and his home and his honor.

"With a pistol, every man is his own king."

The pistol is not so much seen these days. And recent Presidents have been lawyers.

(I think the pistols are still around but are tucked under the coat in the pistol pocket.)

When you do see them, they are ornate affairs—the American .45 automatic is the most popular.

The grips are made of silver and gold or carved ivory.

The barrel has been nickeled to mirror brightness.

"Let me tell you a story," said the man from Acapulco. "While I was running a hotel down on the coast, I had a man working in the kitchen as a dishwasher. The fact that he had a big .45 tucked in his belt was no matter. We all carried pistols.

"He was a good man and I promoted him to waiter.

"But he still carried the pistol, you see. He was very polite—he was a good waiter. He kept his white jackets clean.

"But he would come to the tourists' table and say, 'What is your command, Señor? The shrimps are good today.'

"The tourists would take a look at this man with that big pistol stuck in his belt. And they would turn white! I tell you, they would say, 'Anything you suggest. Yes, of course, the shrimps.'"

"I told him, 'Man, you must take off that gun you are wearing. You frighten the tourists.'

"I said, 'At least, man, don't wear the gun in the dining room.'

"He said to me: 'Then, Señor, you must put me back in the kitchen. Let me go back to washing dishes. Would you ask me to go around without pants?'

"He said: 'Let me go back to the kitchen, *patrón*. For truly I cannot live without my love. Without my pistol.'"

Anyone for Tennis?

Mexico, D.F.—I telephoned Hertz for a car. Hertz is pronounced "Airtz" in Mexico—as Avis is called "Ah-vees."

"Airtz de Mexico," said the voice. It sounded brisk, efficient. Even encouraging.

Five years before, the maneuvering to rent a car took two days and nearly drove me off my rocker. Airtz sounded more like business this day.

"I wish Hertz to put me in the driver's seat—as the ads say on TV," I said.

"What kind of car do you wish, sir?"

"A compact. How about a Falcon?"

"Ah," said the Airtz girl triumphantly, "we have no Falcons. Only Opels."

"I will take an Opel."

"Very well," she said, "just a moment."

The phone cut out and switched to another line.

"Airtz de Mexico. *Reservaciónes.*" Brisk. Right with it. Everything clicking.

"I would like to order a car—an Opel."

"Certainly, sir. When do you wish it?"

I said tomorrow. *Mañana.* No use pushing these

things. I even hummed a little tune. When I thought of the last time and those unending two days—

"Just a moment, sir."

The line switched again. "Airtz de Mexico."

"I want to order a car—an Opel."

This voice sounded a little harried. She said: "Certainly, sir." Then she said, "I cannot talk to you now."

"Why not, Señorita?"

"Because we are getting a long distance call."

The line cut out completely. I dialed the number for Avis. "Ah-vees de Mexico." Would Ah-vees try harder as the ads say?

"I would like to order a car—an Opel."

"We do not have Opels. Only Falcons."

We established that I would take a Falcon. Tomorrow. At 12 o'clock punctually. "I am leaving town and must have it promptly."

"Have no fear, sir. The car will be waiting."

It seemed odd that Hertz would be the ones to put me in the Avis driving seat. But this is Mexico—

At noon, I had the bags down and tipped the bellboys. At 10 past, I phoned Ah-vees. I explained that the car had not come.

"Did you reserve a car, sir?" (That is a bad sign. When

papers get lost, you have to start all over again. That is how I spent two days. Five years ago.)

I explained that I had. The Ah-vees man wanted to know if I had reserved standard shift or automatic. Standard, I said. He sounded doubtful. Most Americans take automatic.

"The car will be there in five minutes."

I let the five minutes drift into half an hour and phoned again.

"Ah-vees de Mexico!"

"About my car—it was to be here half an hour ago."

"Did you reserve it, sir?"

We established that I had a car on order. True.

"What has happened, sir, is when we took your car to the garage for gas, something is wrong with it. We have no more Falcons with standard shift."

I asked what Ah-vees proposed to do. To try harder? Or were we going into another two-day waltz? "Would Hertz have a car?"

"Oh, yes, sir." He sounded grateful. "Hertz has many cars."

"On the other hand, why don't you send me a car with automatic shift?"

"In five minutes, sir."

And within one more hour, the car was there. Showing how much things have improved in the car rent business. It used to take two days. Now it only takes two hours.

The City Changes

Mexico, D.F.—A light haze hangs over the Valley of Mexico in the morning. Partially because much of Mexico still cooks on charcoal. Turning out the rich corn tortillas which, stuffed with mashed beans and flavored with hot sauce, are a better breakfast than ham and eggs.

The streets are lined with flowers. The fountains run— thanks to a former Governor of the Federal District. (If you have seen the breakdown of plumbing in the back country, you will recognize the miracle here.)

Steel-and-glass skyscrapers climb into the Mexican sky. Adding more altitude to Mexico's breath-taking 7300-plus feet.

"Man," said the waiter, "the siesta is something no one

thinks about anymore. We are all modern in Mexico these days.

"We are more modern than New York," said the waiter proudly. "For one of our clients came back only recently.

"He said to me, 'Man, you would not believe it. But in New York I took a siesta each day. First,' said our client, 'everybody in New York goes to lunch at noon. But they do not eat. No, man, they drink the martinis.

" 'You drink one martini and your friends say, "Now one more."

" 'Then they say, "One for the road."

" 'Next they say, "I can't seem to get any work done at the office. Let's have another."

" 'At the end of the lunch, you go back to your hotel and fall into bed.' "

Said the waiter: "That is why we are more modern than New York. Here we have no siesta."

Even Franco in Spain was not able to end the Spanish custom of the siesta.

But Mexico City has lost the habit. Little by little, in the last 30 years.

The stores that once closed for several hours in the warm afternoon, are open. And air-conditioned.

The street repair crews lunch and return to the pick.

The taxis go rushing through crowded streets.

"I recall when Mexico City went to bed in the afternoon," I said. "A most civilized way of life."

"Me, too," said the waiter. "But now we are advanced. We get heart trouble. And the most modern medicine to cure it. It is more civilized than the siesta."

"For our clients," said the waiter. "we have diets without salt if they wish it. We have little pills instead of sugar.

"In the old days, the clients came to me and said, 'Pepe, give me a little *pozole* for the hangover and a glass of mescal.'

"They said, 'Pepe, for the love of heaven, bring me only a tequila and a little strong soup.'

"Now," said the waiter, "they come back from New York. They say, 'Pepe, bring me two martinis and a tranquilizer. Also I have a new diet and cannot eat salt. Open a can of the diet soup and bring me the salt-free crackers.'

"It is extremely modern. The latest thing. We import only customs approved by the most up-to-date cities. Heart problems from the United States. Liver troubles from Paris."

"On weekends," said the waiter, "we took the waters at Ixtapán de la Sal. It cures the gout. And if one was sterile, he had only to take one glass of the water—! Miracles!

"Now our clients play golf on the weekend—Mexico City has the finest golf courses, they say. Though I do not play myself. It is two hours to Ixtapán. And they must prepare to be

at the office early Monday morning.

"Diets and golf. Traffic and tranquilizers. Two martinis and soup without salt. Thus we grow. If one wishes the siesta, he can go to New York, no?"

The Dust of Mexico

Mexico, D.F.—*"Once the dust of Mexico has settled on your heart, you will find peace in no other land."*

Once the dust of Mexico has settled on your shoes, you will find no peace from the shoeshine boys.

There are hundreds of shoeshine boys in Mexico City. In every Mexican town, there are dozens around the shady plaza.

In Mexico City we get our shoes shined several times a day.

"Shine, Señor?"

"I just had them shined, *muchacho*."

"But look, Señor."

What has happened to the twin mirrors I had a half hour ago? A half hour ago I had them shined in a sunny courtyard. A soothing beginning to the morning. Black coffee. The gentle "swish-swish" of the brush.

The shoes came out brilliantly—I could have sold them for double what I paid for them.

I took a short walk in the Alameda.

The shine disappeared. The shoes look worn and run-over. I should send them to a charitable organization.

In the lovely park, fountains sparkle and children play. A balloon man holds a great bunch, globes of all colors tugging him to heaven.

Once the Holy Inquisition burned heretics here.

Processions of masked priests marching in the street. The victim in chains. The spectators mad with excitement. Some of them broke through the guards and pleaded with the chained man to repent before the fiery death.

It is sunny on the bench. I might as well have another shine.

On the street behind us, the taco sellers are dishing up fragrance. Steaming meat and tomatoes and chilis wrapped in a tortilla. (Cortez and his men ate them—the recipe has not changed.)

The shoeshine boy gives the shoes a final swish.

"*Listo*, Señor. Done."

What magnificence! You could put the shoes on the table and see well enough to shave!

With shoes like these I must go to some elegant place for

lunch. (Too bad I can't put my feet on the table.)

The shine lasts exactly one half hour. Cinderella shoes. Back to the chimney corner.

It's our last day in Mexico City. For awhile. For a little while. I always come back. The dust of Mexico has settled on my heart.

Besides, there is no place in the world where you can get such brilliant shoeshines. So often.